# The Legacy of Inherited Wealth

## INTERVIEWS WITH HEIRS

*Edited by Barbara Blouin*

*& Katherine Gibson*

FOREWORD BY ROBERT COLES

*Revised Edition*

TRIO PRESS

T RIO  P RESS

P.O. BOX 933, BLACKSBURG, VA 24063-9533  540/953-3977
IN CANADA: 6940 TUPPER GROVE, HALIFAX, N.S. B3H 2M6  902/429-2235
http://www.inheritance-project.com
Trio Press is a wholly owned subsidary of The Inheritance Project, Inc.

9 8  7 6 5 4 3
Revised edition

*Printed in the United States  of America*

CANADIAN CATALOGUING IN PUBLICATION DATA
Main entry under title:
The Legacy of Inherited Wealth
ISBN 0-9699195-8-1

1. Children of the rich — United States — Interviews.
2. Inheritance and succession — United States.
I. Blouin, Barbara, 1940-    II. Gibson, Katherine, 1959-

HQ799.97.U5L44 1995    305.5'234'0973   C95-950029-4

*Dedicated to
all the inheritors who
shared their lives with us*

# Contents

*These names are pseudonyms.*

# *Acknowledgments*

With special thanks to Meg Federico, who was a co-founder of
The Inheritance Project. We are deeply grateful for her vision,
enthusiasm and generosity. Her ideas helped give shape to this
book, as well as to much of our other work.
Thanks also to Robert Coles, John L. Levy, Denny Blouin, Dee Hall,
Emily Sell, Hazel Bercholz, Liza Matthews, Suzanne Townsend,
& Andrew Glencross.

# *Foreword*

These are stories of men and women who have been challenged by (and who, often enough, have chosen to challenge) the wealth that has become theirs by virtue of inheritance. Put differently, they have been born to the bright promise of money, but have also learned that such a lot is not without plenty of potential hazards, if not outright dangers. It is, I fear, all too easy for many of us who have never faced this particular kind of situation to be somewhat skeptical of its significance, the very real threats it can pose to any number of individuals. Time and again, in my clinical work as a psychiatrist, I have heard my patients bemoan their various troubles — and then insist that if only they had more money, things would somehow work out. I have listened, and marveled at the simplicity, the naiveté of such a conviction — not, I hope, out of a smug and arrogant condescension on my part, but out of my experiences as a child psychiatrist who has worked with poor children and rich children both, and who, so doing, has learned that yes, money can indeed solve certain problems (those that are connected to its lack), but that families with plenty of money can also be (though, of course, not necessarily) quite troubled and confused and hurt. Moreover, money is itself such a vexing matter to so many of us in a world so sensitive to both its presence and absence that it can generate its own kind of difficulties for people who may seem to have everything, but who know full well, often enough, what they don't have, or yearn to have more plentifully: affection, self-respect, membership in a community of neighbors or fellow citizens or colleagues at work, those bonds that are, yes, priceless.

As I read these candid and poignant narrative accounts, I was reminded of a girl of nine I got to know in the course of my work, actually, with "privileged" boys and girls, as I described them when I wrote up the research: privileged to live "comfortable, comfortable lives," as that girl and several others kept saying, when I asked them to tell me of their days, their ways. Such a summary, however, was a mere beginning — as that girl, soon enough, let me know: "People think we have everything in the world you could ever want, but that's because they've forgotten to look right in the mirror at themselves." When I heard those words, I have to admit, I wasn't at all sure of what this youngster was meaning to tell me. I let her know that — asked for some clarification. She was generously forthcoming: "Well, you see, these people who say they'd like to be rich, so then they won't have anything to worry about — I'll bet a lot of what they worry about won't go away, even if they become as rich as can be." She stopped for only a second or two, and then reminded me that her sister had a serious illness (leukemia) that no amount of money could banish, that her mother had struggled for years with a so-called "nervous condition," and that her dad was a relatively isolated man who was all too suspicious of all too many people (whom he believed were out to fleece him of his abundant financial resources).

The girl didn't describe the foregoing aspects of her family's life as I have just done; she simply said that her family had "these troubles," and "money won't fix them," and then she mused that others, too, had troubles that weren't going to be resolved by infusions of cash: "If you get sick, and it's serious, then you hope you'll get better, but you can't write a check to make yourself better!" She'd heard that, naturally, at home — even as she'd realized on her own, living in a particular home, how lonely her father was, a consequence of his money-connected suspicions. No wonder she once told me she thought she might be much happier were she poor. She knew to have second thoughts on *that* score, too — knew that poverty, like wealth, brought no necessary earthly salvation. As I tried to learn from the statements, the self-portraits that follow in this book, I realized how helpful it had been for me to know that child, to receive her wisdom, earned in the course of a brief but eventful life, even as I suspect the readers who go through these pages will also feel themselves a bit more knowing and alert to this life's ironies and complexities.

In a sense, what follows is a series of morally introspective self-confrontations: people given much by fate trying to figure out how, in turn, to give to others — the great summons for all of us. No matter who we are, what our background, our means, we are ultimately affirmed by how we live our lives — with and for whom we spend our time, our energy. Here are fellow human beings who have been trying ever so hard to find for themselves a purpose in life, a direction for their energies — and here we are, their readers, given a chance to learn of them, of course, but most important of all, to learn from them. Each person's story, after all, can ultimately become part of our own — can offer us lessons that we can absorb, lessons that thereby can help inform our lives. These are seekers; they want to put certain advantages of luck to good and proper use — and so it is with each of us, for we all have our various gifts and talents to offer, and we all need to know, through the example of others, how to do so — how to connect in mind and heart and soul with others near and far.

ROBERT COLES

# Preface to the Third Edition

We offer this revised edition with gratitude for the steadily growing interest and support we have received since 1995, when we first published *The Legacy of Inherited Wealth*. The changes we have made reflect some positive developments in our work and in the field of wealth management.

First, two of our interviewees have decided to substitute their real names for the pseudonyms they used in the first two editions. The fact that Barbara Stanny ("Sarah Stein") and my co-editor, Barbara Blouin ("Deborah Frank"), have chosen to reveal themselves marks, for both, a movement beyond shame into a fuller acceptance of inherited wealth as a positive part of their identities.

Second, we have revised and expanded our resource directory. The alterations we have made reflect not only the usual gamut of changed addresses and phone numbers, but also the expansion of services and publications now available to wealthy families and individuals throughout the United States. In the past few years, many of our readers have found this directory useful in locating resources to help them with issues of wealth and inheritance. We hope that with its updated information and new listings, our resource directory will continue to be a valuable guidepost for heirs and their families.

Finally, we want to acknowledge feedback that some readers have offered: that reading this book left them feeling depressed. A few of the narratives in this collection are, indeed, sad stories. Even though the rest of the collection is more upbeat, all those we interviewed had their struggles and sometimes felt unable to deal with them. To be frank, this book is a reflection of what we heard in talking with more than forty inheritors.

Taking seriously our readers' feedback, however, we have decided that it is important to collect stories from inheritors who have found

— or forged — more successful relationships with their inherited wealth, with their families, with their friends, and most of all, with themselves. To that end, we are gathering some inspiring stories for another book. Our aim is to provide models of emotionally healthy people who have discovered empowering and socially useful ways of handling and passing on their wealth. We hope this next book will generate fresh ideas about how the inheritance process can be managed with grace, compassion and wisdom.

KATHERINE GIBSON
*April 1999*

# Introduction

*The Legacy of Inherited Wealth* explores the emotional consequences of inheriting wealth. The inspiration for this book springs from the personal quests of its editors. As heirs ourselves, we struggled for years in isolation to come to terms with our wealth, both of us longing for someone to talk to candidly about our private conflicts and confusions. It was wonderful to find one another. We met in 1992, quite by chance, through a mutual acquaintance. Over a chilly winter weekend at Barbara's home in Halifax, Nova Scotia, we drank tea and started sharing the details of our lives as inheritors. We haven't stopped talking since.

The isolation we experienced is altogether common. Money is such a taboo subject, and talking about inherited money is especially taboo. Many heirs feel cut off not only from one another but also from those who do not share the experience of wealth. Our main purpose in compiling this collection of stories is to break through the isolation, challenge the taboo, and give our readers a sense of community. Nearly everyone we interviewed told us how relieved they felt to speak openly about what it is like to receive family money. We hope this book offers the same relief to other inheritors.

If there is one accurate generalization we can draw from these interviews, it is that abundant wealth has a way of separating heirs from the grist of life. For some inheritors, this separation manifests as a painful inability to identify their real needs and longings. More than anything, such heirs are searching for ways to bridge the distance they feel from themselves. Other heirs find it difficult to establish authentic and trusting friendships; they worry that perhaps their net worth matters more to friends than their self-worth. Still others find it hard to connect with meaningful work, often not knowing how to take the first step toward developing a gratifying vocation.

1

And the list goes on. A number of heirs told us how out of touch they are with the management of their assets. Some feel acute embarrassment and "fogginess" when confronted with the practicalities of their wealth. On the other hand, there are those who have plenty of financial knowledge but lack the joy of a heart-centered philanthropy. When heirs cannot connect their ample resources to a meaningful social vision, giving away money can feel empty, like a mechanical obligation. Finally, we met several inheritors whose experience of disconnection is all-pervasive. One described it as feeling like a spectator of life, perched always "on the periphery" of things.

For readers who find themselves wrestling with similar kinds of problems, we have provided a comprehensive resource directory at the back of the book. In it are listed support networks, conferences, wealth counselors and therapists, books, and newsletters — all geared toward the thousands of people who face challenges as inheritors of wealth. We encourage heirs who feel confused, overwhelmed, or paralyzed by their wealth to take the first step of contacting one or more of these resources.

Our approach in this book is purely personal. No surveys were conducted, and no statistics were compiled. We found our interview subjects through a network of friends and acquaintances, relying on phone calls, home visits, and word of mouth to reach our fellow heirs. As a result, we do not regard these interviews as research but as a collection of intimate and moving human tales. In short, *The Legacy of Inherited Wealth* offers a view from within rather than a view from without.

We interviewed more than forty people, all of whom contributed to the shape and direction of this book, regardless of whether or not we finally used their stories. The seventeen men and women whose narratives appear here range in age from twenty-three to fifty-seven, and come from every region of the United States. All but four asked to remain anonymous, so we have given them pseudonyms and changed other identifying details such as their hometowns, schools, and names of their family members and friends.

As we spoke with heirs, it became clear that each person's sense of wealth is subjective. An inheritance of a million dollars seems like a fortune to some, yet it is a drop in the bucket to others. So we decided not to define "wealth" in terms of a certain income level. For the purpose of this project, "wealthy" means having enough inherited money to make paid work a personal choice rather than a necessity. Although many have chosen to do so, none of the people in this book needs to earn money.

We met with most of these heirs for at least two hours, sometimes returning later to finish our conversations. A list of the kinds of questions we asked appears at the back of the book. We began by asking heirs about childhood experiences, but before long, most interviews took their own course. The conversations veered toward the subjects each heir felt most passionate about — the mixed messages of *noblesse oblige*, the challenges of marrying someone who does not come from wealth, the frustrations of undervalued volunteerism, the enforced ignorance of some female inheritors, the potential divisiveness of family business, the disillusionment of being used by friends, and so on.

The sequence of these stories requires some explanation. The early ones reveal a good deal of inner turmoil; to some, they may seem bleak, especially when read together. Further on, however, the stories become more hopeful as they focus on the process of personal empowerment and financial education. The final narratives are inspiring examples of inheritors who have beautifully integrated their wealth with their social visions and their spiritual values. For one heir, in fact, this meant giving away his entire inheritance.

We chose to order the interviews in this way to reflect our belief that real wealth has very little to do with money and almost everything to do with living a creative and useful life. It means minimizing guilt, which can paralyze heirs, and maximizing our resources, both innate and given. To that end, we regard the process of investigating the effects of inherited wealth on our lives as a central task for heirs. Becoming conscious of how our inheritance may have held us back is a necessary prerequisite to envisioning how that same wealth might allow us to make a real difference in the world. Our book traces this path from the pain of ignorance and shame to the pleasure of positive creation.

We see *The Legacy of Inherited Wealth* as valuable not only to heirs, but also to the professionals who work with them. Because it illustrates in such detail the challenges of inheritance, this collection is an excellent resource for financial, legal, and therapeutic professionals who want to enhance their relationships with wealthy clients. It can be hard for those without inherited wealth to imagine, never mind to appreciate, the realities of a lifestyle that is often glamorized way out of proportion. This book is an effort to demystify the experience of inheritance for professionals so they can better understand and communicate with clients who come from wealthy families.

This book is helpful too for readers who are neither heirs nor professionals who work with heirs. Here are vivid accounts of struggles to which anyone, wealthy or not, can relate — struggles for independence, self-respect, love, and purpose. These stories challenge our culture's most cherished myth that wealth brings happiness. Instead, the inheritors who so courageously open their lives to us in these pages show that they suffer just as others do. They teach us that wealth is no vaccine against pain, and that happiness is a product of right living rather than financial ease.

We trust that all our readers will come to this material with open minds and hearts. As editors, we run the risk of presenting material which could fortify our culture's preconceived notions about "the rich." We are also, however, deeply attuned to the psychic damage that stereotypes create by denying people the dignity of their individuality. So we encourage our audience to listen for the individual voices — pained, searching, or enthusiastic — amidst this chorus of heirs. In so doing, they can help to dismantle stereotypes which, in the long run, harm us all.

We want to stress that not all families find the transfer of wealth as difficult as those of most heirs included in this book. Especially in families in which parents are comfortable with their wealth and in which children are well prepared to receive family money, the process of inheritance can be truly empowering. This book, however, is intended as a service for heirs who are grappling with the emotional dilemmas of their situation.

Many of the heirs featured here come from families who, in varying degrees, suffer from dysfunction. In some cases, having wealth exaggerates the family's underlying problems; in others, the wealth itself is perceived as the source of family troubles. But in both cases, the transfer of money from one generation to the next poses

4

significant challenges for the heirs with whom we spoke. For this reason, we have selected interviews which describe the journey or the lack thereof out of isolation, embarrassment and impotence.

Finally, we would like to make two comments about neutrality. First, it is our view that money itself is not the real problem for heirs. Although our culture vacillates between enshrining money as the source of all happiness and condemning it as the root of all evil, money is actually just a neutral medium of exchange. It does, though, have a way of highlighting people's difficulties. As one heir succintly puts it, "Money is like a snowball; it collects all your problems." It can be liberating to recognize that wealth is not the ultimate cause of every unhappiness we experience.

Second, we harbor no judgments about the personal decisions heirs make regarding their wealth. In short, as editors, we have remained politically neutral. Although as individuals, we believe in using our wealth to mend and enhance the social fabric, we do not want to risk making other heirs feel guilty or inadequate if they do not share our values. Guilt and low self-esteem plague too many heirs as it is.

Our only agenda is to encourage heirs to increase their awareness about the effects of wealth in their lives and the lives of others. Ultimately, we believe that as heirs undertake the gradual process of exploring and resolving their personal blocks around wealth, the natural result is an impulse to generosity, a desire to put one's resources to use for the good of others. It is this conviction that undergirds our whole philosophy about inherited wealth.

BARBARA BLOUIN & KATHERINE GIBSON
*January, 1995*

# Sophie Carlson

*Sophie Carlson came of age feeling disconnected from her heart and from her body. Isolated by her family's affluence from the choices and crossroads that most people face, she rejected her parents' lifestyle and became a janitor in a shopping mall. After several years, Carlson got a toehold in life's basics — working for a living and learning how to stretch a dollar. She now realizes that she must somehow return to her family and the heritage she was given.*

The household I grew up in was filled with people. There was our family of eight, and then there was the phalanx of mercenaries who ran our lives. We had cooks during the week and different cooks on the weekend, we had a laundry lady, we had some people who didn't come on a regular basis, and we had a nanny. Pearl was kind of an upstairs maid. The laundry lady, Esther, had worked for our family for as long as I can remember. Her parents had been slaves. We had a handyman named Jake who had Parkinson's disease. He was kind of wiggly. He cut the grass, painted the back porch steps, hosed down the driveway, and washed the cars. We had a chauffeur to drive Dad around after he retired.

Nanny was white, but no one else was. When I was very small, I thought that when you got older, you turned black and worked in a car wash. I remember asking my grandmother, "Well, when are you going to turn black?" She seemed awfully old to still be white.

Nanny had worked for our family for thirty-five years; she had taken care of all my father's children, so she was quite old by the time she came to me. Her name was Penelope Axe, and she wore a white uniform and a cardigan, with the top button always fastened under her chin. I thought Nanny was my personal property. Nobody else could command her attention and time. The other kids had had to relinquish her to me. She was my person in a household that was filled with lots of people.

Nanny left the summer I turned five. I'm sure my mother tried to explain it to me, but I couldn't comprehend whatever I was told. I asked Mom, "When is Nanny coming back?" and Mom said, "Nanny isn't coming back." At first I couldn't believe it, but I remember the moment I finally understood: I was standing in the kitchen, and the sun was setting beyond the driveway. I could just burst into tears right now! Nanny had left some of her clothes, and I used to sit on the floor of her closet and rub them against my face. When Nanny left, I lost a whole reference point. I had always looked for her when I came into the house. Who was I going to look for now?

It wasn't just that Nanny left, it was that I suddenly realized that all those people who spent a lot of time with me did so because we paid them. And if we didn't pay them, they would go. It was a haunting notion. I also thought the help could be fired. I got the idea that they could be fired if they did something I didn't like, and I would run around the house screaming, "I'm going to fire you!" Can you imagine how insulting that was, to have your employer's pre-schooler running around yelling, "You're fired!" I'm sure Mom punished me when she found out. I guess I was trying to understand how the relationships worked: If I was powerless to command their love, perhaps I did have the power to threaten them with the loss of their jobs.

My father worked every day except Sunday for most of his life. So I think we didn't see ourselves as wealthy; we saw ourselves as upper class. If you saw our house from the outside, you wouldn't think it was ritzy, but it was big. There were twelve bedrooms. We drove Buicks and Fords, I wore hand-me-downs, and my father didn't spend money on himself. He told me a story about the first time he bought something he didn't need. My parents were in London on business, and my mother talked him into buying a Liberty silk bathrobe. It's hard to explain: there was a difference between "quality," which was seen as good, and "ostentation," which was crass.

You could characterize our family life by saying that we were enormously verbal. We talked about everything all the time. If someone wasn't talking, people thought they were coming down with the flu. There was a rule that we had to have conversation of general interest at the dinner table. We couldn't talk about personal details, like what we had for lunch. We used to talk about ethics, politics, abortion — big issues. I had a lot of siblings, and we had to fight for the floor. And once we got the floor, we had to hold it. You got a lot of points for being the wittiest and the most devastating.

When the civil rights movement started to be in the news a lot, when that issue made it to the dinner table, I realized that all our help was black. It made me uncomfortable. I began to feel the social separation that our wealth conferred on us — on me. I remember once my mother had opera tickets she couldn't use, and she arranged for Camille, one of the occasional help, to take me to the opera. I was mortified that people would know that Camille wasn't simply taking a friend to the opera; she was a black woman being paid to take a little white kid. I wasn't embarrassed that *she* was black, it was the other way around: I was embarrassed that *I* was white.

Then there were all the assassinations — John F. Kennedy, Martin Luther King, Bobby Kennedy. Those events had a big impact on me, but because I was a child, I couldn't articulate a political position. All I could do was feel upset and confused. I noticed that things were unjust and unfair, yet I knew I couldn't fix them. I felt it wasn't okay that we had lots of money and other people didn't, but I didn't know what to do about it. I still had to sit at the dinner table and make conversation.

I was becoming savagely cynical. I thought my parents were hypocrites. How could people go to church when other people were being killed? How could you sit in the comfort of your beautiful home and watch the fucking news without re-evaluating yourself? How could you sit at your dining room table and dip your fingers in the finger bowl when there was a war in Vietnam? I see now *I* was being hypocritical: the civil rights movement and the war in Vietnam were convenient covers for my rebelling. Did I really care, or was I just pissed off? Who knows?

I fell in with an older crowd. It was 1968. Everybody had read Tom Wolfe's *Electric Kool-Aid Acid Test,* and we were second-generation rich suburban hippie teeny boppers. We weren't old enough to be in protest marches. All we could do was absorb the consumer end of the whole media hype about the counter-culture — drugs, bell bottoms, rock music, and granny glasses. And on top of that, of course, hate our parents.

9

I felt horrible about my life. I developed bulimia, which people are hip to now because of Princess Diana, but believe me, they weren't then. I was a real wreck. I had no communication with my parents, and I had no compassion for them whatsoever.

If I close my eyes and go through the houses in my neighborhood, I can see some kind of tragedy in each one. There were sons and daughters who drank themselves to death, who beat up their parents, who ended up in jail or in mental institutions. There were sons and daughters who disappeared, never to be heard from again. I think those terrible things happened partly because the parents' world and the childrens' world were two almost separate spheres, with few intersecting points. The kids were extremely bored and confused. We were supposed to create a separate society identical to our parents' society, but on an adolescent level. We were supposed to have tennis dates and drink tea in the afternoon, but we wouldn't do that. And because we wouldn't do that, no one knew what to do with us. We children were not proud of the fact that our parents had money. I was ashamed. It was a confusing time.

I was such an ungrounded person, and the affluence permitted me to become even more ungrounded. My life was turning into an out-of-body experience. I was reading the French Surrealists and Celine's *Journey to the End of Night* and listening to the Velvet Underground. I was wrapped up in my head. Nothing else mattered to me; nothing else touched me.

Having so much money added to my sense of groundlessness and contradiction. I was alienated from the simple business of ordinary life. I felt no necessity to do anything. I couldn't see why anyone did anything. I felt that I had nothing to look forward to. I was not moving towards a future that I could imagine. The only thing I was looking for was a way out of the suburbs.

I couldn't see my place anywhere out there in the world. I couldn't identify with working-class people; I didn't even know any. I couldn't identify with the civil rights movement because we had all these black people working for us. The world of wealth and privilege was surrounding me, and I felt I couldn't reach out and touch anything real. There were too many choices and not enough consequences. I didn't have to do well at school. Nobody could flunk me out; my uncle had donated a huge new building.

10

I think my parents were at a loss what to do with me. There they were, providing me with all the benefits my father had worked so hard for; he didn't take a Saturday off for forty years, and I was throwing everything he had worked for in his face. My parents didn't understand what they'd done wrong.

My mother did a great thing for me. She got me a job as a volunteer at an emergency children's shelter. I worked with children who had been burned with scalding water and beaten with extension cords. The state would intervene, break down the door, serve the parents with papers, and whisk the children away. My job was to to play with these battered kids and take them to their dinner. The place was dismal. It was connected to a hospital by a tunnel, and we would walk the kids through the bowels of these old, crumbling buildings, full of hissing pipes, with one bare light bulb every twelve feet. The kids would eat in the hospital cafeteria — if you can imagine anything more grim than that. When they'd finished their canned ham slices and instant mashed potatoes, I would bring them back and help get them ready for bed. Then I would drive off to my comfortable home.

Working with those children and with the staff put me in touch with the real world. I discovered that I could actually do something. I began to be connected to my own sense of basic goodness, basic worth. I wasn't just a gigantic brain full of turmoil and confusion, driving my body around like a rental car. I could actually do something that was fundamentally good. I could hold those children on my lap and let the simple warmth of my body comfort them.

When I was eighteen, the summer I graduated from high school, I left home. I went to California. My dad wanted me to come back at the end of the summer and go on to college, but I didn't do that. The day I left, my head was almost shaved, I had on Frye boots, a black polyester halter-top dress, a blue-jean jacket with ACE spray-painted across the back — because that's what I wanted people to call me — and a knapsack. My parents took me to the airport. I remember them standing there, looking old and sad.

And that was it — not even a backward glance. When Mom realized I wasn't coming back, she sent my trunk with a bunch of weird junk in it: school uniforms, blankets from camp, and my teddy bear, which I still have. I was living in a sort of crash pad — a rooming house with a communal kitchen, two communal bathrooms, a pay phone, and the most incredible roach infestation you can imagine.

That was when I started to get my inheritance. My mother and father decided to give me the income from my trust fund. I had no control over the principal, thank God. So I had my own money, although it wasn't a lot — around $650 a month. At first I argued, "I don't need your money!" and Dad pleaded, "Oh, honey, just let me send it you. You don't have to spend it." It's quite painful to remember: I was talking to him from the pay phone, the traffic from the main drag was roaring in the background, and he was begging me to let him send me money.

I didn't want the people at the rooming house to think of me as an incompetent, useless, rich person, so I got a job as a dishwasher, which lasted about two weeks. I also did a stint as a cleaning lady. Then I got a job as a janitor in a shopping mall. Those were interesting experiences for me; it was the first time I had worked for a paycheck. Every morning I dragged myself out of bed at 5:30 and caught a bus to the mall. The only other people on the bus were a bunch of mentally handicapped adults who lived in a group home just behind my rooming house. They all had jobs like mine. We would disembark in the empty parking lot just as the sky was beginning to lighten. I used to help one guy, Ray, who was easily the size of a linebacker. He mopped floors at a Burger King, and without my guidance, he would have gotten lost in the warren-like corridors of the mall. I used to pick Ray up after work too and lead him back to the bus stop.

We janitors worked a thirty-six-hour week, which meant that we were classified as part-time, so we got no benefits. We were paid minimum wage. We spent each and every day vacuuming the endless acres of industrial carpeting that blanketed the floors of all the stores in the mall. When we weren't doing that, we were wiping fingerprints off of a thousand mirrors and three thousand chrome garment racks. We got one fifteen-minute break a day — just enough time to scarf down a sandwich. The sales clerks were instructed not to speak to us or acknowledge us in any way.

I felt good about that job. It was like, "Yeah, I am a regular person. I am willing to pull my own weight, and I'm not proud. I'm capable, and I'll clean the toilets. I don't think I'm above anybody else just because I have money." I took a lot of pleasure in letting my father know that I was working as a janitor and cleaning up other people's messes. I think he always figured I'd outgrow it. He had tremendous faith in me.

Looking back, it seems odd to me that I had such an attraction for menial work. Maybe it was because the people who had taken care of me had done menial work. When I was little, I was in a good position to observe. I remembered watching Ida rolling out biscuit dough, using a juice glass to cut round shapes. I remembered tiny leaves of bright green bibb lettuce floating in a huge white enamel sink while she fixed salad for dinner. She could pare an apple and keep the red ribbon of peel intact every time. I remember watching Esther stir the blue laundry starch for Daddy's shirts on a big old gas stove we had rigged up for her in the basement. I remember watching Pearl rub mayonnaise on a water ring on the dark mahogany dining room table. I remember dust mops, cleaning rags, pails full of vinegar and water. My memory is inhabited by people doing this kind of work.

I'll tell you a story. My friend Sheila had a mother who was not too interested in mothering. Sheila was raised by the housekeeper, Bradley, who cooked, cleaned, mended, and generally did everything a mother is supposed to do. When Sheila's mother decided to have the family portrait painted, she made Bradley go to the sittings in her place. Bradley would hold Sheila on her lap. So there in the portrait was Sheila, in Bradley's arms, with her head resting on Bradley's bosom, looking lovingly into Bradley's face — except that it isn't Bradley's face in the picture. Right at the end, the artist painted in the mother's face above Bradley's neck. Then the mother had the gall to complain that the picture never looked just right!

The hired help take care of you, wash your clothes, make your dinner, wipe your nose. Yet it is hard to acknowledge the role they've played in your life. They don't come to your birthday party unless they are serving the cake. I ran into Sheila about five years ago, after her mother died. She told me that she had gotten back in touch with Bradley, and now she visits her, sends her money, and generally takes care of her. So Sheila has been able to acknowledge that Bradley actually nurtured her. That nurturing is not something that you can just pay for. If you have been raised by other people, it is so important to feel that it wasn't just a job for them, that real life was happening, and real, honest love. And it's so important, later on, to find a way to thank them for their love.

I also gravitated towards physical work because it brought me into my body. One of my best jobs was working on a construction crew, banging nails into sheetrock. At the end of the day, I was so tired I couldn't think, but it was satisfying to see the walls of a building going up around me. Laboring for a wage and using my paycheck to take care of myself helped me connect money and living. That was how I got connected. You can't just buy your life without putting some of yourself into it. You risk becoming completely disconnected; you don't have a real relationship to anything. But it took me a long time to identify the wealth itself as an issue.

The first time the money came up as a big issue in my life was when I got married, at age nineteen, to Bruce DeLong. He had been in prison for several years for protesting the war in Vietnam, and I met him not long after he got out. Can you imagine anything more romantic for me? He was twelve years older than I was, and he was incredibly slim and handsome. He was so kind and gentle to me. He was a hero — a real man of principle.

Bruce came from a big working-class family in Minnesota. His father worked in a factory. They were the kind of people who clipped coupons and shopped sales. Every kid had his chores, his part to play in keeping the family going.

I wanted to get married because I thought it would make life with my family better. Instead of living with somebody, I'd be married to somebody. Well, of course, it wasn't better; it was just awful! I had no idea what was involved in the statement "We're getting married." My entire family were there — about fifty people. It was as though someone had transplanted them from the golf club and stuck them on a jumbo jet. There they were, with their martinis in their hands, smack in the middle of my counter-culture life. I mean, none of my friends even had socks that matched! Bruce's family had come on the bus — a long ride. His mother was the sweetest person in the world; she had a puffy hair-do. The kids were wearing party clothes from Sears. We had our wedding at a meditation center, with everyone sitting on cushions on the floor, except for the parents, who were sitting on flimsy folding chairs.

I remember my father telling me, "You know, your getting married to Bruce is one thing, but meeting his family is the last straw." He had never met people like that, unless they worked for him. The whole scene just went from bad to worse. It was so embarrassing, humiliating, and excruciating.

Mom had sent out wedding announcements, and then all these fancy gifts started pouring in. I used to cry every time UPS delivered something. I would open up the box, and there would be a silver tureen. I had absolutely no idea what I was going to do with it. Bruce would come home, and I'd be sitting on the kitchen floor amidst a blizzard of Styrofoam peanuts, crying as I unwrapped another demitasse cup. That was when I started to realize something about how money creates differences between people. I mean, Bruce's parents lived in a one-story house with all those kids. My family, on the other extreme, were from the American version of "Masterpiece Theater." It was awful for me, and it must have been awful for Bruce. And it was hard on both our families.

We were living in a tiny house, and Bruce's sister and her husband moved in with us. That was when my money really started to stick out. Brenda and Chris were really struggling; they couldn't rub two dimes together. I had jewelry in my bureau drawer and a fur coat in the closet, and they were living on hot dogs. I was getting money from my trust fund, and on top of that, at Christmas, my father sent me two certificates of deposit for $10,000 each. He was trying to get the money out of his estate. I opened the letter, and there was $20,000. How was I supposed to relate to it?

I hadn't realized how sensitive people are about money. I didn't understand that your economic status in the world is connected to your social worth and your self-worth. I guess I thought everybody knew that when you were born, you were born into circumstances that were beyond your control. If you were born black, it wasn't your fault, and if you were born poor, it wasn't your fault, and if you were born rich, it wasn't your fault, either. It still surprises me that the world isn't like that; I still find it shocking that people blame you for that.

The contrast between my assumptions about life and Bruce's assumptions about life was becoming painfully clear. I was starting to see through my masquerade. I was never going to turn into the stoic Bruce DeLong. And I didn't need to live the hand-to-mouth lifestyle

I was parading around in. My father wasn't a factory worker, and my mother didn't buy clothes at Sears. We did clip coupons, but we gave them to the help.

I had figured out who I wasn't, but I still had to figure out who I was. Without my costume on, I felt pretty naked. Bruce and I got divorced after a year or two. We didn't split up because of the money, we got divorced because we were about as incompatible as two people could be.

I began to consider what growing up in affluence had given me. I had been given the tools to make it possible for me to move in any social circle that I might choose. People who are trying to come up in the world often have to overcome their backgrounds, but if I wanted to go up, I had nothing to overcome. It's only when I want to go down that I have to hide my upbringing. Denying who I was was creating a kind of psychic friction, and it was a relief to stop acting. All the same, my years of cleaning the mall and pounding nails had given me the chance to connect with my body, with other people, and with the million minute details of ordinary life.

I moved back East, I went to college, and I tried to reconnect with the past. I had to take everything I had experienced and sound the depths until I could chart my own course. Eventually I remarried, and now I have a family of my own to raise. My father used to say that you only notice what your parents did wrong, not what they did right. So each generation is condemned to make the opposite kinds of mistakes. My parents had so many demands made on them that family life wouldn't have been tenable without the hired help. My family life has unfolded differently, as have the times. Thank goodness I am not raising children circa 1968!

My own lifestyle, which I feel comfortable with, has taken a while to synthesize. I don't want my children to see me paying other people to make our lives possible. We have somebody who cuts the grass, but we don't have someone who cleans the house. I don't want a nanny, although I tried it out for a few years. I don't want to hire any more people. I want my kids to know that you can feel good when you clean the bathroom, that there is nothing demeaning or unworthy about taking care of yourself. There is dignity in the simple business of washing your clothes, cooking, cleaning, and taking out the trash.

Your body, which you have to take care of, is the starting point. Everyone has to do that. There is strength in knowing that you can care for yourself, that you are capable of meeting your own basic survival needs. Then you can develop the strength to help others. If your wealth comes in between you and the nitty-gritty basics of living, you can miss that connection.

# Rebecca Hutchins

*As a young adult, Hutchins was plagued by a sense of aimlessness. Paralysed by shame over her wealth, she drifted for years. Eventually she set herself a physical challenge to give her life a positive focus: she became determined to do the Ironman Triathlon. In achieving her goal, she discovered that she could rely on a strength that had nothing to do with her money. In addition, she learned to respect herself.*

I had a pretty happy childhood. I grew up in a big, rambling house in Massachusetts, out in the country, with several acres of woods and fields. My father was a writer, but he never made much money from selling his writing. He had a little income from his family, but for the most part, he lived off my mother.

When I was eight, our family moved to Jamaica for four years. We had a beautiful house with a big lawn and a pool. We had a lot of Jamaican friends, and my mother and father didn't try to separate us from them. My parents never said, "You can't play with them. You are different, and it is not appropriate." Instead, the message was that we were all kids, and kids like to play together. Every day, our new friends swam in our pool and played soccer and marbles with us. They even came to some of our birthday parties. I give my parents a lot of credit for being so liberal-minded. Living like that, I saw incredible contrasts. Some of our best friends were the gardener's children. There were six children in that family, and they lived by our gate so that he could open and close the gate for our car. They had a tiny two-room house. From time to time, I'd spend the night with them, and I remember sleeping on the floor on a little straw mat.

Every summer, during all my growing-up years, I would go to Whale Island off the coast of Nova Scotia, where my grandparents had a huge summer house. The extended family owned most of the island, and there were several family houses besides my grandparents' house. My aunts and uncles and cousins would come in July and stay for the rest of the summer. My grandparents' house was on a hill overlooking Chester Basin. My great-grandfather, William Theodore Chandler, built that house. It's enormous. I mean, it just goes on and on. A few times, I have taken friends up there — friends who did not have the kind of money I have — and I felt embarrassed. You take one look at that house and you practically faint.

Three times a week, all the grandchildren would be invited to the Big House for dinner. I had to put on a dress, and my brothers had to wear coats and ties. We always complained about that. "Are we going to the Big House for supper? What a drag! Oh, Mum, do we have to get dressed up?" We would go for cocktails at six. Grandma was very tall and slender, and she would be dressed up in a nice dress with perfume on. And Grandpa would have khakis on and blue sneakers and a button-down shirt and a jacket. Cocktails would go on for maybe an hour, and then a maid would come in and say, "Dinner is ready." We would all go into the dining room, and the table was set with silver and a white tablecloth, and Grandpa would carve the meat. He would sit at one end of the table, and Grandma would sit at the other end. And when the first course was done, Grandma would ring a little silver bell, and someone would appear and start clearing away the plates. And then we would go on to the next course.

The family owned a twenty-four-foot sailboat. Races were held twice a week, so there would be dinner-table talk about "Who is racing next Thursday?" and "All right, we'll go out in the Boston Whaler and watch the race," or "I'm going to play tennis tomorrow at the Yacht Club, and maybe I can call so-and-so, and we'll get a doubles going." It was all very proper and polite. Looking back, I really miss those days of spending time with my grandparents, that whole routine and all those traditions. It was a real constant in my life. After Grandpa and Grandma died, the Big House and the other houses were divided up by my mother and her siblings. I still go to Whale Island every single summer, and there are many uncles and aunts and cousins and nieces and nephews around. The style is much looser and more casual now. Everyone has their own house, and people get together and have picnics on the beach. But it is no longer like it was in my grandparents' time. They were at the top of the pyramid, they were the patriarch and the matriarch, and that was reassuring and comforting for me.

My parents divorced at the end of our time in Jamaica, and we moved with my mother to North Carolina, where I lived for a handful of years. I went to a large public high school where there was a lot of cheating on tests, and I cheated too. I did almost no homework. I smoked in the bathroom, I started using make-up, and I shoplifted underwear with my best friend. I began sneaking out with my friend, meeting boys at midnight and getting drunk with my friends. Then I went away to a girls' boarding school in Connecticut — Miss Porter's. It was a wonderful experience, and I blossomed. I didn't have to worry about boys and dressing up for them or wearing make-up. I did about three hours of homework a day, I was on the varsity field hockey and lacrosse teams, and I was a member of the student council. I felt very safe and contained at that school. I was also aware that only certain people could afford to go to boarding schools. It felt like we were somewhat elite, the cream of the crop. We were privileged.

When I was a senior, I began to overeat. My food addiction got worse and worse, and I felt a lot of shame about it. I didn't know it was an addiction; I didn't have a label or a context for it. I had no idea why I was overeating. After boarding school, I went to the University of Michigan. These were my expectations: a) I was going to lose the fifteen pounds I had gained senior year at boarding school; b) I was going to party and have a great time; c) I was going to get a B+ average, or better, without making much effort; and d) I was going to fall in love with a great guy. That was my rosy picture.

But none of these dreams came true. Those were the most unhappy years of my life. A big university was much too anonymous for me. I had gone from one extreme to the other, and no one seemed to care about me. I didn't have any family nearby, and the contrast was too great. I gained more weight. I think I had at the most two dates in four years of college, and they were with guys I didn't even like. I worked my butt off, but I only had a B or C average. I was depressed, I was a loner, and I felt like I didn't fit in. Fraternity and sorority rushes were happening, and I tried out for a sorority. I don't know why I did that because I just hated it. I thought I should wear make-up and be pretty and be in a sorority and go to football games. But all of it seemed so alien to me, and I wasn't very popular. I don't think any sororities even considered taking me. And then I thought, "Wait a minute — I'm an elite person. I come from the East from an aristocratic family with lots of money, so how come things aren't working out the way I expected?"

After college I moved to L.A., and for six months I lived with a black man, a struggling musician, and he really snookered me. I bought him music equipment, and I paid for his recording sessions. I will never forget the day he spent $700 on a suit without asking me. It turned out he had a wife and children on welfare in Kansas. I also found out that he had another girlfriend, and he also had children by her. I'm embarrassed to say that over a ten-month period, I loaned him about $20,000. Of course, I have never seen a penny of that money.

After that disaster, I was feeling somewhat lost, and I didn't know what to do careerwise. I decided to go to nursing school at UCLA, but I ended up not liking it. I was still in my loner mode. I went to the gym, and I went to movies, and I studied hard. I was cut off from myself and very unconscious. I was just going along. Every summer, I went to Europe and backpacked alone. I really liked doing that. I have been to Europe about fifteen times. I hardly ever tell anybody that because I am embarrassed about having done so much travel. For five years, I went to Carnaval in Rio. I fell in with an international crowd who went there every year. I see in retrospect that Carnaval is an alcoholic scene. People get drunk and go crazy. I now understand that I was recreating my alcoholic family dynamics.

After I graduated from nursing school, I still did not know what I wanted to do. I was afraid to settle down to a nine-to-five job; I just wasn't ready to join the establishment in L.A. I dawdled. Then I decided that I would like to work in Africa. I wanted to find a short-term position over there, either paid or voluntary. My plan was to work a little bit, and then travel around Africa. Then I would come home, get serious, and get a "real" job. It was just at that time that a famine broke out in East Africa. I still had not decided where to go and what to do. I had not put anything together. So I decided to go to Mozambique and pitch in. I remember talking to a man at one of those third-world aid organizations in New York. I said, "Well, you know,

I have not been able to get anything, so I think I'll just buy a one-way ticket and go over there and show up. Do you think I'll find a job that way?" He was very rude to me. He said something like, "Are you kidding? No one is going to hire you if you show up on the doorstep! What a ridiculous idea. Don't waste my time. Goodbye!" I ended up buying a one-way ticket, and I went over to Africa without a job. I had two travel books on East Africa, and forty-five minutes before landing, I opened one of the books to the chapter on Mozambique. I was really winging the whole thing.

I had intended to be there for a couple of months, and I ended up staying just over two years. I started as a volunteer in a famine relief camp for four months, and then I was asked to stay on. It was an extraordinary experience. I did a variety of jobs — everything from being out in a rural area to help with food distribution to working at the headquarters. Then I was put in charge of the orphan program. Later on, I was put in charge of redesigning the famine relief camps away from an emergency focus to a long-term development focus. While I was in Mozambique, I felt completely inadequate — an imposter. I thought I was going to be found out any day; someone was going to discover that I didn't know what the hell I was doing.

I fell in love with an Australian. Our relationship lasted a couple of years, and it was very powerful for me. I felt that this man taught me how to love. When we had vacations, we would meet each other in different countries. The only problem was that he was married. Eventually his wife found out, and he sent me a horrible letter that she had made him write in front of her and the children. When I read that letter, my heart crumbled into a thousand pieces.

After that, I didn't have a clue what to do. I had been planning on moving to Sydney and living with him, and now I had to come up with Plan B. But I didn't have a Plan B. I felt so lost — alone in the world with no plan or direction.

I have had inherited money ever since I can remember. I get dividends from my grandfather's trust. They come in the mail periodically. To give you an idea of just how out to lunch I am about this, I never know when those checks are coming. And I never know what the amount will be. I am always sort of surprised when I get a check. "Oh, look, another check for $7,000!" And two days later, there will be a check for $6,000, and I'll say to myself, "Oh, another one so soon! What do you know! I just got one!" I actually remember saying, dozens of times, "Ugh! More money!" The feeling I had was that the money was already such a burden and a weight, and when another check came, there was even more! Often I wouldn't even deposit those checks for weeks. I'd just do it when I got around to it.

I'm quite unclear where the money actually comes from. I let other people handle it, and I hardly know what I have. All I know is that I have between $2 and $4 million. It is very fuzzy and hazy to me. I have kept myself in the dark because it has been too overwhelming, too intimidating, and too much of a painful area for me.

I am not proud of my ignorance; it is very embarrassing to me. I think what underlies that ignorance is an enormous sense of shame around having inherited money. The shame has kept me paralyzed in many ways, primarily in the area of work, which I am now beginning to move through. I am just beginning to talk about my shame. In fact, this past weekend at a Haymarket conference for people of wealth, I led a workshop on shame. It gave me an opportunity to talk about my feelings with other people.

The shame of having tremendous amounts of money which I didn't earn has made me not want to reveal my ignorance. Whenever I went with my brothers and sisters to meetings of the extended family, or whenever we met with lawyers or financial planners or tax people, I would seldom ask questions. I would just play along, pretending I knew what was going on. I would nod my head and say, "Well, that sounds good to me," and "Oh, do you think that is the way to go? Let's do it that way." I have followed on the coattails of my three older brothers and various male cousins, who are quite involved and interested in family financial matters. They understand business stuff, and they take part in it, which I have not done. And I am not interested in doing so. It bores me to death, and I am embarrassed that I am bored by it. I feel like I should not be bored, that I should be grateful and act responsibly with my money, but I'm just not there yet.

I also feel embarrassed and ashamed because I know so little about the family business. I think I have blocked out the information. All I know is that the family money has come down through several generations on my mother's side. It started, I think, with her grandfather and got built up more by her father. He left millions of dollars in trust to all his grandchildren, as well as lots of property in Chicago.

My three brothers, my two sisters and I have a family lawyer in Manhattan. He is a really wonderful and unorthodox kind of lawyer. Sometimes we have lunch with him, and I have met his wife and kids. I trust him, and I rely on him in many ways. I have a very complicated tax situation, and when tax time comes around, I would not even know where to begin. Nor do I have any interest in doing my own taxes. There is a man in New York who handles my taxes, and I have never spoken to him. I can't even remember his last name. I collect all the stuff that comes in the mail, anything that says, "Taxes for the previous year" or "Save this for tax time." I put it all in a manila envelope. I don't even photocopy it, which I'm embarrassed about. It just seems like too much to photocopy, and I get stuck emotionally. At the beginning of April, I send that off to my lawyer, and he photocopies it and sends it to my accountant.

Every year I seem to need an extension for my taxes. My return never seems to be in on time. I don't know why, but it always ends up happening, and at some point, months down the road, I get a letter in the mail, a bill for $2,000 or $3,000 for the fee to have my taxes done. And I get a copy of my tax return sent to me, but it is lengthy and complicated, and I don't even read it. Or sometimes I skim it, but I don't understand it. And then I put it away, and that's it for another year.

Around that terrible time when I lost the love of my life, I read *Women Who Love Too Much*, and it became a catalyst for major changes in my life. That book totally hit home with me. I realized, "Oh my God! I come from an alcoholic family! Oh my God, this is why I have been involved with so many older men who are father-figure types and who are unavailable." I started to put the pieces together, and I began to see my father more clearly. I had always bought into his grandiosity. I saw him as a Hemingwayesque figure — a romantic artist. He would stay up until three in the morning, drinking and talking about politics and literature. My friends used to say, "You have the coolest father!" But they never saw his other side: when he got really drunk, he could be insulting, and he would sometimes attack us verbally. I have a lot of shame about growing up in an alcoholic family, and that adds to my shame about my money. All of a sudden, I had a context for understanding why, for so many years, I had been depressed and lonely and disconnected from myself and other people. I finally understood why I had been a binge eater, why I felt so lost and empty. It explained the huge, black void I had felt inside of me for ten years or more.

I also realized that I was not alone, and that there were things I could do. I could go to twelve-step programs like Al-Anon and Adult Children of Alcoholics. It was just what the doctor ordered. I spent about a year and a half making my recovery as an adult child of an alcoholic the top priority of my life. I meditated for an hour or two every morning. I attended ACOA meetings twice a week, and Al-Anon meetings once a week. I went to a "Women Who Love Too Much" support group every Saturday. I just gobbled it up. I was learning, I was growing, and I was applying all the tools that I was learning.

During this period of active recovery, I understood that I had gone into nursing because I wanted to take care of people, mend people, and I realized that I didn't want to be a nurse. That decision only added to my confusion because I really didn't know what to do.

Right around that time, something else was going on that ended up changing my life in a big way: I began training for my first triathlon. The summer after I returned from Mozambique, I did the first of two twenty-six mile swims from L.A. to Catalina Island. I joined a masters swim team, and I went to three workouts a week. I biked two hundred fifty miles, I ran fifty or sixty miles a week, I lifted weights. Ever since college, I had wanted to do a triathlon. Somehow, I had an intuitive sense that I could do it, so I decided to go for it. I think wanting to do a triathlon was very much tied into my money. I needed to prove to myself that I could do something great — just me and my body and nothing else. I had been in recovery for some time, and I was much healthier emotionally. I discovered that I could ask for support, which I had never been able to do before.

I decided that I would ask a trainer I knew if she would coach me, and she said yes! So I did intensive training six days a week for nine months in preparation for the big event — the Ironman Triathlon in Hawaii. During those months of training, I went to Nova Scotia, where my family spent their summers. I biked the whole length of the Cabot

Trail in Cape Breton — those magnificent, rugged mountains. I swam around Whale Island, as well as a few other nearby islands. It was a wonderful feeling; this was where my roots were. When I was born, Grandpa and Grandma had a boat built in my honor, and they named it the Rebecca Leigh, after me. My full name is Rebecca Leigh Hutchins, and to this day, that boat is still around. It is not a pleasure craft; it is a work boat, even though it is not actually used for work. It is very sturdy, and I like to think that I'm as sturdy in the water as that boat has been all these years.

So there I was, travelling through the waters of Nova Scotia on my own. Like the Rebecca Leigh, I would swim by a playhouse that you can actually walk into, and I would swim by a beautiful chapel that my great-grandfather, William Theodore Chandler, had built. There are plaques in the chapel that say things like, "Abigail T. Chandler was married to James P. Greenlaw on such-and-such a date." I would swim through seaweed and around lobster pots. It was an incredibly good feeling.

In October, 1985, I competed in the Ironman triathlon. I had asked some of my family to be there to support me, and they came along. My mother and my stepmother and one sister were there, and one of my brothers, a passionate photographer, took pictures. I think you can sense the contrast from my lonely, depressed college days: here I was, accomplishing my dream, with all this support. I want to make the point that it took me fourteen years to realize my dream of doing a triathlon.

I had a great time. The weather was perfect, and everything went well. I was really well trained, and I was totally psyched. I was going to make it, come hell or high water. Only an act of God could have prevented me from finishing. I did the Ironman in twelve hours and twenty-three minutes. I saw my family clapping and yelling, "Bravo! Bravo!" It was incredible!

Then I went back to L.A. and enrolled in a program to become a drug and alcohol counselor. I knew a lot about addictions because I came from an alcoholic family, and I was very familiar with twelve-step programs. The program was related to nursing, and I believed passionately in recovery. I did two internships during that program, and I remember that the staff at both places couldn't understand how I could afford to be an intern and not have a paying job. I knew the day was drawing near when I had to get a paid job. Enough was enough — interning, volunteering, going to school, escaping through travel, and whiling away my time weren't satisfying any more. I was a master at hiding out, looking good on the outside while feeling totally inadequate on the inside.

Around that time, I fell in love with Alice, my coach. We decided to live together, and we moved to Providence, Rhode Island. I had always been heterosexual, so I was really caught by surprise when I found myself attracted to a woman. Alice and I are still together, five years later.

I was still totally paralyzed workwise. I definitely mean "paralyzed" because that, more than any other word, describes how I had felt about my work life ever since I had graduated from college. I was totally stuck. I literally didn't know how to find a "real" job, although I did know how to get work in a restaurant. You just walk in, you say, "Can I waitress here?", you meet the boss, and you're in. But in my entire life I had never gone through the process of putting together a resumé or going through a formal interview and being judged and scrutinized, and either hired or not. I think my ignorance about how to get a job was very much connected with my class background, although I can't identify exactly how. Ever since I can remember, I have known that I would not have to earn a living if I didn't want to. Knowing that left me feeling trapped and unable to breathe. I had been trying to climb out of that trap for all of my adult life, but I couln't find a way out.

I longed to do work that I could feel passionate about. I'm completely envious of people who are clear about what they want to do, and then they just go ahead and do it. "What do you do?" is my least favorite question in the entire world. I loathe that question. I'm very good at bullshitting. When someone would ask me what I did for a living, I used to say that I was in graduate school. That sounded good, and it got people off my back. Then I would say, "I'm in training for the Ironman." That sounded okay for a while, too.

I'll tell you what made the difference for me in getting a job: I recruited Alice to become my job coach. She had been such a wonderful triathlon coach that she and I came up with the idea that she could tutor me in how to find a job. We worked out a system:

27

every Sunday afternoon, we would have a little work meeting. We'd sit down with a spiral notebook, and we'd write down anywhere from three to seven tasks for me to do in the coming week. It started off with unthreatening, do-able, simple things. And as time went on, the tasks got harder and harder, like, "Do a mock interview" or "Write a draft of a cover letter" or "Begin looking through last week's newspaper and cut out ads" or "Sit in your meditation room and visualize the job you want." Every Sunday for three or four months, we did these exercises. I'm embarrassed to say this, but it really helped. And every Sunday, before we came up with the tasks for the next week, Alice would say, "All right, Rebec, did you do such and such?" And when I said yes, I would get a sticker. We had lots of sheets of stickers that said things like "A-Plus," "Way to go," "Super," "You did it," "Well done." I was just like a little kid.

What made the difference for me was having someone holding my hand throughout this process. The goal of finding a job, which until then had seemed completely overwhelming and paralyzing, was broken down into about fifty little manageable steps, and I did them, one at a time. Over a period of two and a half months, I sent out nineteen resumés. To my absolute amazement, nine agencies called me in for interviews. And of the nine agencies that called me in, four called me back for a second interview. And one of those agencies actually offered me a job. I was bowled over! I had been thinking, "There are so many gaps in my resumé. I'm not marketable. No one is going to hire me." And when that job was offered to me, I felt like a kid: "Oh my God, I am marketable! I am marketable! Me, Rebecca, apart from my money!" My money did not buy me the job. None of the people who interviewed me even knew that I had all this money behind me.

Getting a job was a breakthrough for me, a real going forth into the world. I have been working now for over two years at an agency near Providence, and I enjoy my work. I work in a community health center. All of my clients are very low-income, and it is a real eye-opener for me. Since I started this job, I walk taller, I feel so much better about myself. I am really proud of myself. And I am a kinder person and more patient. I have noticed all those changes in just over a year. Some days as I am driving to work, and it's a pain to be stuck in traffic, I think, "I am going to work. I am dressed up. I am going to work." I look around at the other people in their cars, and I think, "Isn't this great? I'm just like everybody else. At last I am normal." I only make $24,000 a year. I get a check twice a month, and it is for seven hundred and some odd dollars. It is peanuts for me, and I can't imagine how anybody lives on so little money. But I look at that check, and I am so proud of it. I earned it!

If you are a wealthy person reading this book, I would say that the thing that would probably be the most helpful, as it has been for me, is to get whatever support you think you need. Come out of hiding at least enough to consider joining an organization. Hook up with other people who are in your shoes. Talk about money issues. If you can't talk about money with family members or friends, go to a wealth conference. I went to my first Haymarket conference in the fall of '89. It was an all-women's weekend conference. I was blown away by the experience. I felt like a dam that burst — I just flooded. Forty years' worth of emotions and shame came barreling out of me. And now I am beginning to come out of hiding about my money. I am beginning to tell more people, people I feel safe sharing this part of myself with. People need a forum where they can talk about their wealth issues with other people who will hear them and accept them right where they are, and who will not put them down or intimidate them.

It's not as if I don't still have a long way to go. To this day, I have not been able to start dealing with the technical aspects of my money. I know next to nothing about how to manage my money; it's still too intimidating for me. Right now I am working on my emotional issues around money — money and work, money and shame, money and relationships, money and family. Eventually, I plan to find out exactly how much money I have and learn where the different amounts come from. I would like to get a history of my money, and I hope it will sink in instead of going in one ear and out the other. Eventually, I imagine I would like to take far more control of my money. I think I would like to get out of the joint ownership situations with my siblings and cousins, and I'd like to consolidate and simplify my financial picture.

But for now, I'm happy because I'm unstuck, I am working, and I am finally beginning to integrate my money into who I am instead of disowning that part of myself. I've opened the door of the trap and have stepped out. I'm on my way.

# Henry Baldwin

*Henry Baldwin has always lived the same lifestyle as his wealthy parents. Now, however, in his mid-thirties, he has begun to wonder whether being free of worries about "the mortgage payments and that sort of thing" makes him different from other people. Although he enjoys and respects his privilege, he is beginning to question the facade of happiness he feels compelled to maintain. Like many heirs, he feels drawn to explore the messages with which he was raised.*

Beginning in nursery school, I went to private schools where most of the kids appeared to be in the same economic class as myself. There were nice cars in the parking lot — that sort of thing. And as a little kid of six or seven, I started asking questions about money. I had heard about millionaires, so I asked my father, "Are we millionaires?" And my father said, "We're comfortable, but we don't need to get into those details now. The important thing is that we are good people. Having money isn't something to be ashamed of. There are wonderful things we can do with our money."

At twelve or thirteen — at a very early age compared to most people — I was brought into the loop of the family offices on both sides of my family. We did financial planning as a family, and we have done that kind of thing for a long time. Even though I didn't understand much of the detail, I started sitting in on meetings at the family offices and working on allowances and budgets. It was explained to me what the family's investments were, and my parents took me to visit some of the companies we had investments in.

I had a checking account when I was fourteen. At that age, you're not writing very many checks, but I learned how to balance my checkbook, and I learned that the little piece of paper I wrote my name on is just as important as a ten-dollar bill. I learned about the responsibilities that go along with having money. If I had wanted to, I could have written a check for who knows what, but I wanted to do the right thing. I remember talking with my mother about the difference between income and principal, and that sort of thing. My parents were always giving us examples, as we were growing up, about someone who was pulling his money out of such-and-such investment, and he never worked, and he was whittling away his fortune, and pretty soon he wasn't going to have any money left. And they would say, "That's fine, if that's what you want to do. But we think it's better to live off your income and preserve your principal and try to compound it so that you can give away more money."

When I was around fourteen, I received outright one hundred percent of my net worth — no strings attached. I guess my parents just assumed from day one that we were going to be responsible, so they just did it that way. They didn't think they needed to put the money in trust and make us jump through various hoops in order to get it.

I felt very well prepared, and I was never ashamed of having wealth. I've always thought it was a great opportunity. My dad always said that wealth has its advantages and disadvantages, but the advantages outweigh the disadvantages. He said that wealth gives you a wonderful opportunity to do great things, not so much for yourself as for others and for the community. And at a very early age, maybe sixteen, I was encouraged to start making charitable contributions.

My kids are eight and six, and they are learning in school about coins and money. They're at the same school that my wife and I went to. It's more diverse than it used to be, but it's still a fairly affluent private school. My kids fit in just wonderfully. I think my wife and I will do things not too much differently with our kids from the way I was taught. We've been looking for the right vehicle for passing on our wealth to them. We're mostly setting up trusts, but there will be plenty of income going to them when they're still young so that it won't be a situation where the flood gates are opened when they turn eighteen, and they're suddenly inundated.

We took the children on a tour of the bank a couple of weeks ago, and we showed them what a safety deposit box is. Our oldest brought all his coins down to the bank and put 'em in the big coin-counting machine. He traded in all the coins and bills that he had earned over the past year, and he ended up with about $104. So he got a hundred-dollar bill, and he looked at it and he looked at all the coins and stuff that he had collected, and he said he'd rather have the coins. They looked like more money to him, but then he said, "Well, maybe I like this hundred-dollar bill after all."

So we're just starting the process of teaching our kids that we're wealthy, and that we shouldn't be ashamed of it, but that we're not going to live outrageous lives. We have discussions with them, and we talk about how we're lucky to be able to live this way, and we take wonderful vacations, but we don't fly first class. Well, once in a while we do. . . We kind of keep it in moderation, but we don't skimp. We just lead a comfortable life. We're not ostentatious. We have comfortable houses — even fairly amazing houses — but we don't live a flashy lifestyle. We're pretty laid back.

We don't drive the fanciest cars in the world, although I probably had a nicer car than any of my friends when I was growing up. But it was a comfortable car and on the upper end of being nice. It wasn't overboard. Growing up, there was more of that kind of thing — flying first class and maybe being picked up at the airport in New York in a limousine. But as far as day-to-day living, we are not too different from anybody else, although we're comfortable, and we never worry about mortgage payments and that sort of thing.

I've got a car collection, and because cars are symbols of monetary whatever, that's seen as pretty outrageous in my family, but it's accepted because it's what I'm interested in. And we have a big piece of property. It's a major commitment, with the upkeep and all that, but my wife and I just decided that we wanted to live on this piece of property. Number one, we want to make sure it doesn't get developed, and number two, it just feels right. And so there are responsibilities with that. We're fortunate that we can afford to do that kind of thing.

My parents also taught me that whatever you do, you should do it well, whether it's volunteer time working for nonprofits, or 80-hour weeks working for some company. There was clearly a message from my parents that if you don't work, you're a bum. And I have a very hard time not putting on a coat and tie and coming downtown five days a week. I feel horrible guilt if I take a Tuesday off to play golf with some friends. I do that maybe once a summer. So I've learned a real strong work ethic, and I'm trying to figure out where I fit in, for myself, in terms of that work ethic. I can make my own decisions, I have my own little office here, and I can come and go as I please. But I'm here five days a week. So it's been interesting to do something with my time and learn or help or be creative or whatever. My parents always taught me: Whatever you do, don't stay home and do nothing.

I was also taught, since I was eight years old, that we have a certain responsibility to the community, and we'd better give. I've enjoyed living here in Milwaukee, where our family has a name and is recognized. We've never moved away. My brother has moved, and I've got lots of cousins who live all over the country for various reasons, but I feel very proud of our name and what our family has done in this area. There's a lot of expectation to fit in — to give to nonprofit campaigns around town, and geez, that "We all do this, so you should do it, too" kind of thing. I don't look at it as pressure, but there are certain kinds of things where you fit into the mold that society has out there. I think the biggest challenge is to try to live your own life, even though you may have certain expectations that are handed down to you.

We're very wealthy, and we're awfully fortunate, and we shouldn't complain about anything. So you've got to hold your head high and not let anything get to you. There's a little bit of having to live the part, and everybody's human and has things going on, but we aren't going to show any of that. A couple of days ago, I talked to a friend of mine who's going through some changes, and he said, "I never thought you had any problems because you've got all the money in the world, and I just assumed money solved everything." And I said to him, "Here's what I've been working on, trying to figure out this and that." And he said, "Boy! It makes me feel great that you're working on things that I'm working on, and it doesn't matter whether you've got money or not." So all of a sudden I realized that I was on some pedestal. Everybody knows I have more money than they do, but I try not to think about it or let it affect me. But it does affect other people — whether you like it or not.

I'm sort of working on not being on the periphery so much, and jumping in a bit more with two feet, which means being more vulnerable. I'm in a men's group with about eight other guys, and one of the guys said to me, "Geez, I don't know you very well. I'd love to know what it's like to have all the money in the world." And I found myself thinking that I don't let people in on some of that stuff, and it may be connected to the wealth, but I haven't figured it out yet. I'm not used to exploring those feelings because everything on the outside has always looked great. And now that I'm starting to get more on the inside, it's still great, but I think there's some things that I have yet to discover. And you grow when you sort of understand all that. And I think one thing with wealth is that no matter what, you look good on the outside. You deny anything that's negative, and I'm not saying there's a lot of negative, but I do know that I'm always optimistic, which you can't be all the time. And I'm just starting to explore some of that, and what the unspoken messages are.

# Barbara Blouin

*Barbara Blouin found growing up wealthy to be a cold and oppressive experience, characterized by distant parents, social isolation and snobbery. Her story illustrates the emotional entanglements of family money, as she discovered that her father's control over his legacy extended even from beyond the grave. Barbara is learning to "own" her wealth and to infuse it with generosity by extending it to others.*

I t's not easy for me to describe the quality of my childhood. I could almost more easily talk about it in terms of what was absent than what was present. Although we had plenty of stuff and all the material comforts, there was no warmth, no fun, no laughter, no friends who came to play, no running around, no comforting messiness. It was as if everyone in the family was walking around inside of plexiglass shields. Other people couldn't get in, and we couldn't get out.

The few photos I have managed to save of myself as a baby and young child show a serious, sad-eyed little girl standing alone or with a nurse. I have no pictures of myself with either of my parents. I was a quiet, obedient, lonely child. I played alone in my room, and I read a lot. Books were my protectors. I stayed out of my parents' way. I took up very little space.

We lived in a large, ornate duplex house that my grandfather and great-uncle had built in the twenties. It had four white pillars in front. Inside, there was lots of dark woodwork, and both the inside and the outside were formal and stiff. There was no sign that children lived in that house.

I don't know how much the oppressive atmosphere I remember had to do with the family's wealth. Maybe my parents would have been cold and formal even if they'd had less money, but I think the money made it easier for them to maintain their hard shields. The money bought them lots of privacy, and it bought my mother all the leisure she could possibly want. Although my parents were usually around at the prescribed times, except for their annual month-long winter vacation, it was really the servants who serviced my brother and me. They drove us around, cooked our food, and washed our clothes. I don't remember Mother baking cookies, and I don't remember either of my parents playing with me. I was looked after by nurses until I was three or four. We also had a series of maids; the one I remember best was a humble black woman whom we addressed by her last name, Mrs. Henderson. Mrs. Henderson didn't speak unless she was spoken to; she definitely knew her place in my family.

Our life was rigid. Mealtimes are a good example: what we ate wasn't particularly tasty — overcooked meat, canned vegetables, iceberg lettuce, and the ubiquitous "Jello." But everything was done with ceremony. Mrs. Henderson wore a gray uniform with a white apron. Lunch was always served promptly at noon, and dinner was at six o'clock on the dot. My father would get upset if a meal was three minutes late. Mother sat at the head of the massively carved mahogany table and signalled to Mrs. Henderson to serve us by pressing a buzzer concealed under the carpet. Then Mrs. Henderson would enter through the swinging door. She served Mother first, and then she would go around the table, serving Father second, always standing to the left.

We also had a grumpy chauffeur named William. He used to drive me to nursery school in a big, black Buick, like a limousine, with two folding seats in the back. Part of William's job was to take my mother wherever she wanted to go because she had never learned to drive. We also had a "colored" laundress. I was afraid of her. Once Mother went so far as to order a maid I particularly detested to wash out my mouth with soap.

Father was a self-made man. His parents were German Jewish immigrants who came over to America on a boat. Father always worked hard, and he succeeded, in his own terms. His company produced glossy colored paper for brochure covers. He used to bring sheets of paper home for me to play with. And he made so much money on the stock market that he was able to sell his business and retire at fifty. From that time on, he spent two or three hours a day reading the *Wall Street Journal* and buying and selling securities. It was all completely mysterious to me. I recently found a letter that he had written in the early sixties, which revealed to me that at that point he had made over two-and-a-half million dollars. He ended up with probably three times that amount, but I'll never know how much because of the secrecy surrounding the money.

Mother was the only child of a prosperous merchant. I think her ambition was to be accepted into the WASPish upper class, but because she was Jewish, she never made it. I guess she got as close to the upper class as she could come in a place like Springfield, Massachusetts. She was on a whole bunch of committees and boards like the Red Cross, the synagogue and the Girls' Club. She went to a lot of meetings. Father was also on a number of boards, and he gave a lot of money to a local college. It must have been an awful lot of money because they named a building named after him — the Joseph Schwartz Center. He was very proud of the plaque with his name on it.

I learned a lot of attitudes about race and class from my parents. Mother and Father never gave out explicit messages, but they were constantly dropping hints and innuendoes. Most of our servants were "Negro" or "colored," as they were called in the forties and fifties. William the chauffeur was Irish-American. My mother spoke disparagingly of "the lace-curtain Irish." It goes without saying that "colored people" were inferior. Mother was always patronizing to the servants. Sometimes, when we were driving through a poor neighborhood, my parents would instruct me: "This is where the Poles live." "This is where the Irish live." We never ate food cooked with garlic because, I was told, Italians smelled of garlic. In fact, I never tasted garlic until I was in college.

One day when I was about nine, I was in the kitchen with Mrs. Henderson, and I found myself wondering if she knew how to read. So I brought her one of my books and said, "I can't figure this out. Will you read it to me?" So she read it to me, very humbly. I think she knew what I was up to, but she didn't let on. Now, when I think about what I did, I'm horrified at my own snobbery.

It was a narrow, stuffy, smug little forties and fifties world I grew up in. School was Dick and Jane and Spot, and I actually thought the world was supposed to be just the way it was portrayed in my *Dick and Jane* readers.

There was an exclusive WASP club in Springfield called the Colony Club, which looked like a neo-French chateau. Jews, blacks, and other undesirables were not admitted. Much later, my parents became the first Jewish family in Springfield to be invited to join the Colony Club. Apparently, the membership had declined, and the directors knew that my parents were wealthy. Mother and Father jumped at the chance.

They were both impressed by status symbols, but at the same time, although they were themselves "new money," they were scornful of the *nouveau riche* a term they used to label anyone they considered ostentatious. There were mixed messages and contradictions all over the place about what was right and proper in terms of one's display of wealth. I remember going to New York with my parents to buy Mother a mink coat at Bergdorf Goodman's. The fur salon was completely lined with mirrors, and it was empty except for two brocaded chairs. Have you ever noticed that the more expensive and exclusive (meaning something which excludes) a store is, the less there is to buy? A few years later, Father bought Mother a second mink coat. I guess he thought the first one was old. However, the message I was given was that we, the Schwartzes, were tasteful; we were not *nouveau riche*.

On the other hand, I sometimes had to wear my brother's hand-me-downs. Although I was told that they were "perfectly good," having to wear a boy's clothes was embarrassing and painful. Although I sometimes wore hand-me-downs, I was provided with all kinds of lessons. There were ballroom dancing classes when I was five, complete with a recital, to which I wore a pink and white organdy dress. There were also ballet lessons, private riding lessons, violin lessons, and piano lessons from a man with a long nose and a gruff, intimidating manner.

When I was twelve, Mother sent me to the Arthur Murray Studio for private ballroom dancing lessons.The instructress was a hard-looking woman with bright red dyed hair and a ton of make-up. She looked like a caricature of a prostitute. I had to dance up close with her, alone in a room, once a week for an hour, for months and months! It was torture. My parents were definitely trying to groom me to make an entry into the upper class, and I didn't dare protest. I was expected to dress like a proper lady and acquire a lady's social skills.

THE LEGACY OF INHERITED WEALTH

Once a year, my parents would take me to New York. Wearing my new spring coat with navy and white checks, my new spring hat, my little white gloves, my girdle, stockings, and heels, I would go shopping with Mother. For a naive young girl from Springfield, it was a big deal. I can still remember the pain from the blisters — I wasn't used to high heels — and the agony of wearing a girdle that cut off the circulation in my legs. I would hobble down Fifth Avenue, admiring the elegant mannequins in Saks and Lord & Taylor. I wanted to look like them. One time, we went to a French restaurant, where Mother wanted to show off my language skills. She said loudly, "Barbie speaks French. Speak French to the waiter, Barbie." I was mortified.

At no time did I get any encouragement or guidance from my parents about how to go out into the world and begin to learn self-reliance. One summer, I wanted to get a job at a Friendly's Ice Cream Shoppe in Longmeadow. It was the "in" thing for teenagers to do. But my parents put an end to that aspiration; they considered it degrading for me to sell ice cream. I was allowed, instead, to volunteer at the Girls' Club because Mother was on their board.

I was raised in such economic security, comfort and ignorance that I was twenty-one before I even thought about preparing myself for life in the real world. I went to Wellesley College, partly because Mother had gone to Wellesley, and partly because my parents had driven me around the campus when I was ten—a smart move on their part. I fell in love with the neo-Gothic buildings and the lake. Halfway through my senior year at Wellesley, I realized, "Oh my God, I'm not going to be here next year! What am I going to do?" I went to the placement office to see what I could do with a major in French and was given some brochures to look at. An organization called the Central Intelligence Agency was interested in training people in exotic languages like Swahili. I was so ignorant that I didn't even know what the CIA was.

I decided to go for a Ph.D. in French because other alternatives seemed somewhat distasteful and because I hoped to meet the right kind of husband in graduate school. Father was paying my tuition, and I had a generous allowance. It seemed so simple. I never thought about what I was doing with my life. I met the man who became my first husband at a graduate students' mixer, and for a long time after

40

that, I thought I was living a fairy tale. Charles was handsome and brilliant, and our very first conversation was about Proust. What could be better? Everything was happening just like I had been programmed to believe it was supposed to happen. I wrote my dissertation on symbolic space in Flaubert's novels, and two weeks later, I gave birth to a son. Perfect timing, perfect life.

Then my brilliant, handsome husband, who had gone on to an excellent teaching job at an Ivy League college, decided to give up his promising career in order to become a writer. In other words, he expected me to support him while he was becoming a writer, but that was never acknowledged. We moved to the Bay Area, and Charles rented a room so that he could write every day away from me and the baby. And I just let him do it. I don't remember arguing with him or even saying, "Maybe you should be working." Even if I had questioned what he was doing, he would probably have said, "Why should I get a job when we don't need the money?"

I had taught French in college for one year, but after we moved to Berkeley, I became sort of an upper-middle-class hippie drop-out. I hadn't found a job, although I admit I didn't try hard. I had naively thought a Ph.D. would be my ticket to a job, and since we didn't need more money, I just gave up.

I tried to hide my wealth, even from myself. We lived in a small, funky flat. I guess we were trying to keep up with the Joneses. All our friends were hippies who prided themselves on not working, living on food stamps, smoking dope, and decorating their flats with Indian bedspreads and orange-crates. We were spending maybe one quarter of my income. I left the rest to accumulate in a bank and refused to think about it. Charles and I never talked about money.

Father set up a trust for us. I remember the papers coming in the mail and Father telling me where to sign. I didn't even read them; I just signed obediently on the dotted line. I didn't understand what was going on until many years later, but what Father had done was to set up the most inflexible kind of irrevocable trust you can imagine. He had always been into control in a big way. He had made a lot of money, and he used it to gain power over people. I think he was able to justify the way he used money to control people by telling himself — and them — that he wanted to make things "secure" for them and "protect" them. Again and again, he would tell me that he was giving

41

me "all the advantages," providing for my security for the rest of my life. I remember just feeling kind of hollow and lonely every year when he announced that he had given me and my brother a "gift" of $10,000. It didn't mean anything to me, and it certainly didn't make me happy. But I was expected to be grateful, and I always said thank you.

Years later, when I was trying to buy a house, I was unable to get a mortgage because of high interest rates. Father made a one-time-only exception to his own rule that prevented me from using the principal of my trust. He loaned me enough money from "my" principal to pay for the house, minus the down payment, which I made myself. I had to pay back every penny.

Along with a trust, I acquired a trust officer, Horace Hayes; he remained my trust officer for the next twenty-five years. For many years, I never even spoke to Mr. Hayes on the phone, let alone meet him. I didn't want to talk to him; I didn't want to know him at all. I didn't even want to know myself. I was too ashamed of my wealth. The trust company took care of almost everything. Once a year, I had to fill in a form so that they could do my tax return for me, and that was that. I got my $3,000 a month (this was the seventies), and just left it in a checking account.

Then Charles left me, suddenly, for another woman. I was devastated. I felt fundamentally unworthy and unlovable. Somehow I managed to connect Charles's rejection of me with the shame I was already feeling about my inheritance. I decided I would give away all my money. It felt like a big burden hanging around my neck, and I thought that in order to respect myself, I should go out and get a job, like everybody else. I blamed the money for much of what had gone wrong with my life, and I think to some extent, it was true. I finally broke the ice and called Horace Hayes to find out how I could give my money away. Mr. Hayes kindly explained that I was unable to dissolve my trust or give away any of the principal, or even keep the checks from arriving every month. There was no way I could prevent myself from being wealthy. I had been so naive that I didn't know you can't dissolve an irrevocable trust! Or maybe I should say that no one had ever explained my trust to me. I guess I could have given away each check as it came along, but to be honest, I didn't have the guts to do that.

As I see it, there is something wrong with the whole notion of irrevocable trusts. The trust company takes a big cut of my income, and I have no choice about how much to pay them, or even whether I want them to manage my money. Everything was decided for me by my father. The people at the trust company are not working for me, they're working for my father, and now that he's dead, they're working for my elderly and conservative uncle. It feels like Father is still pulling the strings, even from beyond his grave. An irrevocable trust is a situation of split allegiance, and that isn't right. The trust is supposedly for my benefit, but even though I receive the income, I don't "benefit" in the fuller human sense. I am to be treated, indefinitely, like a child, who is not capable of making her own financial decisions. That is what Father wanted, and the trust laws gave him the power to do so. The trust is the instrument of his will.

I also want to share some thoughts about giving and receiving. I recently heard an heir speak of her wealth as a gift. Hearing an inheritance spoken of in those terms, I started to wonder why I had never thought of my own inheritance in that way. Although my father had regularly told me he was giving me "gifts" of $10,000 (which of course gave him sizable tax breaks), I never felt like they were gifts. I saw that I had always resisted the "giftness" of my money, first by not wanting to relate to it at all — by ignoring it and not spending most of it. Then I wanted to reject my money by giving it away. I now understand that I haven't been able to receive what was given to me because the true spirit of generosity was absent, and because in our family, as in all families, money was so tangled up with feelings. And because the connections between money and feelings were so unacknowledged. I am working now to take fuller ownership of my money, to feel like it is mine, and in taking ownership, to share it with others. That means accepting the money, even though I still don't feel good about the way it was given to me. Sometimes it is harder to receive than to give.

## AFTERWORD *April, 1999*

Last fall, after a three-year legal battle, I broke my trust. Having my life managed to such an extent, and for such a long time, by an impersonal and inflexible trust company had always felt like a burden and an insult, but after my original trust officer retired, my situation became intolerable. I was assigned to someone who was both incompetent and hostile.

Seventeen years ago, after I moved to Canada, I discovered that trusts were subject to capital gains tax. The only way out was to break my trust—a prospect both scary and thrilling. What if I tried to break the trust and failed? On the other hand, what if I succeeded? I hired a lawyer, and she and my accountant and I worked as a team. My lawyer said to me, over and over, "It was a terrible thing your father did to you!" She meant that by saddling me with such a trust, he had done me a huge disservice.

During the three years it took to win my case, the trust company even charged me for *their* lawyers. But we won, and now I'm a free woman! I don't have to go begging to a trust officer anymore. I interviewed several money managers who specialize in socially responsible investing. Talking with financial professionals was enormously helpful, and I'm now I'm working with someone of my own choosing — someone who is on my side. I am no longer the captive of a trust officer whose allegiance was not to me but to my deceased father.

My anger hasn't dissipated; instead, it has been transmuted into positive power. I'm coming to terms with my confusion and conflict over money, and I'm learning how to use my money in positive and powerful ways.

# Maggie Lindsay

*As a child, Maggie Lindsay suffered from a sense of danger and isolation. In her family, money was used to gain emotional leverage: wealth was "affection and weapons." She often feels numb and unable to discern what she cares about. Lately, she has begun to see that her fear is holding her back from connecting with passion in her life.*

It feels so arbitrary that I have this money, as if it just dropped down out of the sky and fell on my head. The money has always been there, so that I don't even see any benefits to it. Gosh, I could do anything I wanted. I could lie here on the sofa and be depressed all day if I wanted to. I think it is a huge benefit to have time at your disposal, to have the time to think and . . . gosh, have the time to be depressed.

The money in my family came from my mother. Mom was the daughter of a tobacco grower in North Carolina, and she had an awful lot of money. I don't really know what happened, but it seems like part of Dad's attraction to Mom was her money. Dad's mother said that they shouldn't get married because Dad didn't have a job, and Mom remembers saying to her, "That's all right. I have money." Mom pretty much bought a business for Dad. She gave him a tremendous amount of money, and she still had plenty.

Nowadays, my parents detest each other. They have had separate bedrooms for a long time. Mom and Dad are the type of people who don't want to discuss problems; they like to keep everything light and happy. I got that speech so many times when I was growing up: "Everything is fine, and we don't have any problems. We're just a big, happy family, and let's just forget about it." I'm sure that their whole attitude of wanting to avoid any serious topics has to do with all kinds of weird, secret stuff which is related to money.

When I was growing up, Dad would never talk about his work. He was a workaholic — gone by seven in the morning and back at six. And we had no idea of anything that went on down there at the office. It was a complete secret. Dad loved the business, and he didn't really love anything else. We didn't matter that much to him. We always treated it as a joke, because he could never keep our names straight, or the dogs' names, either. He would say, "Maggie or Carol or Ernest (one of the dogs), or whoever you are."

Mom and Dad didn't talk with us about our money in any kind of helpful way; all we ever heard was how much we did *not* have. I remember Dad sitting at the living-room table paying bills, and when a bill was high, like the air conditioning, he would yell and scream, "Goddamn, Goddamn!" Even the dogs would hide. Dad always communicated to us through Mom. He would tell Mom that we had to cut down on our spending, and Mom would say to us, "Now we've really got to stop this spending. We just don't have the money."

So I grew up thinking we were real poor, even though we lived in a big, beautiful house and we had a beach house and horses and boats. But everyone else at the private school I went to had ranches. I thought that we didn't have a ranch because we didn't have enough money. I remember the time a little girl on the playing field at school asked me what I had done for the weekend, and I felt myself going as cold as ice and saying to her that we had been at the ranch. It was very scary; I felt like I didn't fit in. I was so afraid that the other kids would know I was different, and that I would be left all alone.

I look back, and that is one of the things I can't figure out: How did I not see? I must have had part of my brain turned off. I don't know how I could have walked around thinking we didn't have money when everything was right in front of me.

We lived right down the street from a country club, and every time we drove by it, we would scoff at it. Maybe I am just nipping in with my own stereotypes, but there was a lot of plastic blonde hair in Texas and a lot of jewelry. But our family and our friends were really low key. You would never have had any idea how rich they were. Even though we had boats and horses and two houses, we had them in a very unassuming way. You wouldn't know we were rich unless we told you.

I'm still struggling with those things today. I used to feel, and I still feel, like money is kind of a dangerous thing. It is such a big, loud thing that could get me in trouble, so I need to be very inconspicuous. Mama used to say things like, "I'm doing this to save you from yourself." She used to say that when she didn't want me to spend money on something, or when she didn't want me to go somewhere. Once I wanted to go to New York with some friends, and some of them were guys, but I was not allowed to do that. There was always the warning that I would be taken advantage of for my money, or that I would spend it foolishly. So I learned to be paranoid and expect that people would not be honest with me, and that they would not like me if they felt there was this big difference between me and them.

I went to Vassar, to Mom and Dad's pride. They thought it was important for a girl to have a college degree, but they didn't think that the education itself was too important. They discouraged me from doing the things that I think I might have been interested in, like maybe taking some sociology classes or theater or psychology. And I wasn't good at math or science, so I ended up majoring in art history, which I wasn't really interested in.

When I was in college, I began to feel like I had as much money as other people, or more. I had credit cards, and that was a big deal. I also thought, "I'm not a spoiled kid. I even had to buy my own car!" — which, of course, was a BMW. My parents wanted me to buy that car because they thought it would be a good thing to have on my credit record. But then a friend asked me, "How did you have the money to pay for that car?" and that question short-circuited me. I had never even considered how much the car cost. I felt a lot of shame that I had not noticed things like that. Growing up, I had just incorporated being wealthy into the way things were, instead of not liking it or questioning it. And I still feel ashamed about that.

At Vassar, there was some discussion of class differences, but I still felt safe. I felt like there were more people like me than there were people with less money who were criticizing me. But it doesn't feel safe any longer. I think that is because there are so few people in my life these days who have the amount of money that I do. And I think part of my not feeling safe has to do with the kind of leftist community that I am involved in. I could be projecting all this, but I feel that because I have more money than they do, they are mad! So I try my best to keep out of harm's way. I do a lot of concealing.

After college, Mom and Dad wanted me to marry a nice, wealthy boy who was a few years older than me. Mom wanted me to marry a rancher because she wants to live on a ranch with me. She has always threatened to move in with me when she gets old. She also wanted me to join the Junior League and some garden clubs and have at least one child, and generally do what she and Dad have done. I have chosen a very different life from what Mom and Dad wanted, but sometimes I see that unconsciously I am still exactly the same as they are. I feel like I'm going along a pre-programmed path. Here I am: I'm young (I'm only twenty-eight) and I'm queer and I'm left of center politically, but some of my lifestyle choices are out of synch with my political views. In fact, one of my angry ex's owes me money, and she fiercely accuses me of being part of the capitalist system. I identify much more with the left, and I really believe in the more left principles. Yet maybe I don't believe enough.

When I was in college, I absolutely had to wrestle the money away from Mom. She had control over my checking account, and I had never even thought about it. My credit card bills were being sent home, and Mom would pay them out of my checking account. I didn't understand much of what was going on. So there was this big, huge scene because I wanted to take charge of my money. I just remember Mom being furious and telling me that she had paid for such and such for me, and that I owed her that money. We're talking little amounts, like ten dollars. She uses money as a weapon.

In fact, money in our family is affection and weapons. Mom sort of controls the purse strings, so if she likes you, she buys you what you want. And if she's mad at you, she doesn't. I think I have mostly made her happy. I'm sort of better in the scheme of things than my sister is. Carol has taken a lot of drugs and slept around a lot. We refer to her lovingly as our loose cannon. At least I look right; at least I can talk right. Mom still has a lot of hopes for me.

She also encourages feelings of guilt. She wants to be sure that we feel like we owe her so much that we'll take care of her in her old age. I have so much guilt; I am seventy percent guilt. Recently I didn't have enough money in the bank at tax time because I haven't caught on to this IRS thing that you have to tuck away a third of what you've got and be prepared to pay it out every so often. So I asked Mom if I could borrow the money, and she said, "You can pay me back by taking care of me when I am old." And she wasn't even joking!

It's really easy to get money out of Dad. Once he came to visit me here in Vancouver, and he noticed that my girlfriend didn't have a desk, so he went out and bought her one. On the one hand, it was very generous of him, but on the other hand, it wasn't true generosity. It was just Dad's way of being weird about money. Any solicitations that come to him from organizations, he just says, "Write them a check" — whether it's the National Rifle Association or the Gay and Lesbian Defense Fund. It's just crazy. If you can get up the nerve to ask Dad for money, if you can be blatant enough, you can get it, or at least part of it. I feel really guilty about that. My sister feels so guilty that she doesn't even ask.

I am the same way around money as Mom and Dad. Like with my girlfriend, we have got the problem that I have more money than she does. And it's hard to know what to do when I want to go places or do things, and she doesn't have the money. I either have to go without her or I have to take her along. I have always tended to take my girlfriends along. I still lean towards doing that, although now I am a little more wary of it. In return, I feel like, if money is a part of me that makes me more desirable, more interesting, if I am spending money on her, then I want her to be loyal to me. I want her to be really faithful and look out for me and pay attention to what I want.

Once I went to France with a boyfriend for a year, and he borrowed some money from me. I don't even remember how much it was. We wrote up a contract and everything, and then a couple of years later, his father died, and he got an inheritance. He paid me back right away — with interest. That was wonderful. But then I had a girlfriend who also borrowed money from me, and we did up a contract and everything. But now she is mad at me, and she won't pay it back. I'm so upset about it. On the one hand, there is this voice in me saying, "You know, the money is really insignificant to you. Let it go." But on the other hand, it is so messy emotionally to be taken advantage of like that. Finally, I gave the debt to a collection agency. And I still don't know if I did the right thing.

I am in a relationship now; we have been living together for about a year, and I still don't know what I'm going to do about the money. I'm trying to decide what is the best way to handle the money issues that come up between us. It's interesting — in the beginning of a relationship, it's so much fun because my girlfriends are just delighted. It is so exciting for them to go places and do things. And then, after a while, having all those perks becomes a little more commonplace for them, so it is not so rewarding for me as the giver.

The only people here in Vancouver who really know what I have are my partner and my ex-partners. No one else has a clue. And I don't even tell my partners for about a year. Then it feels so good when I can finally tell them. This is such an untapped subject for me; I don't even know why I do all this guarding. For example, I still have my BMW, and if I have to go somewhere that is kind of low key, I will park it around the corner. I know I could take the bus, but I don't want to take the bus. I just don't want my friends to see what kind of car I arrive in.

If a bunch of us meet at a restaurant, and we decide on a designated driver to go somewhere else, I get all bent out of shape if I'm the designated driver. I can't say, "I don't want to do it because I don't want you to see what kind of car I'm driving." In terms of the way I dress, I really hide my money. I dress so bad! You would never, never know I was rich. I wear the same things over and over. Sweats are my favorite. I like to joke that I dress like a gardener.

I also try to conceal where I live. I don't like to say the name of the area. I say instead, "Oh, I live in Point Grey," and I'm always hasty to add that I live in an apartment. In reality, it's a beautiful apartment. I don't think I've ever seen such a beautiful view of the mountains. And it's a lovely neighborhood — couldn't be better. One time, my cover got blown: I remember a friend getting some silverware out of my drawer and asking me, "Is this real silver?" And I said, "Oh, I guess I never noticed. I think my mother got that for me when I was little." Ugh! I was so ashamed! I felt like I was an inch tall; I just wanted to disappear.

But at the same time, I really depend on feeling special because I have money. It feels very safe. I feel different — on a slightly different plane. I almost want to use the word "elite," but that is not quite right. I just feel safe, removed from something that is scary in everyday life.

## Maggie Lindsay

I am interested in doing volunteering, but I find the organizations I could volunteer for, like the Junior League, to be very child-oriented, and that doesn't interest me. And then I just get stuck. I don't know what to do, so I don't do anything. I don't seem to be able to change my focus and make a little adjustment and go on. I just think, "Oh, I can't do it. I can't volunteer anywhere. I don't fit anywhere." I did volunteer for a year at a band-booking agency after a friend had said, "Why don't you do this?" but there was nothing in it for me. I stayed for a while because what else was I going to do? Finally I just got so tired of it that I left. Sometimes I get interested in something, and I say to myself, "Oh, I'd love to do that," but then I don't quite know how to start. I need an instruction manual for every part of life.

People have told me, "You have everything! You should be able to do anything! Follow your dream." But I am just rooted to the spot; I don't even have a dream to follow. There is a kind of frozenness that extends so completely throughout my life that when people ask me, "What have you been doing recently?" I think, "Oh my God, I don't know! I don't know! Don't ask. I haven't been doing anything — nothing. I don't do anything."

I have done some therapy around this blockage I have about finding out what I love, but the therapy has never been connected to my wealth. Now I'm starting to see how the two are connected: I have all the tools I need to be able to do anything I want. So why aren't I doing what I want? It's because there is this guilt that freezes me, so that I don't even know what I want. Once I was talking about some of this in a women's therapy group. I put it out there that I was financially independent, and someone said, "I wish I was wealthy. I could do so much." And oh, it stings so to hear that! I found myself thinking, "You think you could do so much, and I can't do anything." So I asked her, "What would you do?" She said, "Well, I'd put my mother up in a nice house, and I'd pay all my bills." And I said, "Okay, that's the first five minutes. *Then* what would you do?" You know, she couldn't think of what she would do, either.

Once I was having an interview for a part-time job at a leftist bookstore, and they asked me, "If you had all the money you needed, what would you do?" And I thought, "Oh shit! Not this again! This thing just rides me." So I said, "Well, I don't know what I'd do." But of course, I didn't say, "I'm in that position now." I stayed in hiding.

I have been meaning to figure out my finances. I get about $4,000 a month from the family company and the directors' fees. I also have other little investments that I get checks for, and I still get some tobacco money from Mom's family. I just kind of put all that money in the checking account, and I only count the big checks. I have a financial planner now — I guess that's what she is called — who pretty much has my money in a socially responsible fund, the Calvert Fund. I feel better about it being there. And I keep telling myself, "I want to be on a budget, I want to understand, and I want to put away a lot of money for savings." But I guess I don't want to see how much money I *don't* have. It's funny — I don't quite understand, myself. I think I probably have about $85,000 in the bank, but I don't really know how much comes in monthly. There is a part of me that does not want to know.

The hardest thing for me about having money is feeling isolated. It is like having a plexiglass barrier between me and everything, including myself. I can't find the grounding I need. I feel like I need to decide what it is I love, what it is I want to do. Having money also puts a barrier between me and other people. It is *not* the same, no matter what. When people don't know about my money, when I am the only one who knows, I can act like we are having a regular relationship. But in my mind, there is something different about other people's relationships. So if they don't know about me, they can feel safe enough to go ahead and get close, and I can enjoy the benefit of someone getting close to me, just for the sake of being close to another human being. But I'm not sure that if they knew, they would trust me enough to have a vulnerable relationship. On the other hand, if people don't know that I have money, then clearly they don't *really* know me.

But even if they knew about me completely, it still wouldn't work. There is a woman across the street who, I believe, has the same kind of resources that I have. But even between us, when I have tried to talk about it, she just clams up. So I can't even make a connection with someone like her. I just feel so isolated. I haven't been able to find anyone who is like me — the same combination — young, queer, with resources, and kind of leftist. People who have money aren't young like me. And they are overwhelmingly not queer. Young people might have more money soon, but they are on a whole different track. They are working for their money. I just can't make this combination work.

I work hard on my psychological-emotional self because I come from this crazy family who could never communicate. There were so many threats, and I felt so defensive, and . . . oh, just all this crazy stuff. So I have really tried to test myself to try to learn new ways of connecting with people, but I find that holding relationships together is very hard work.

I also test myself through sports. I really enjoy doing sports. I push myself, and I work through the pain. I go over to the gym and work devotedly on the weights. I never see any gain (I'm puny) but I really try. I guess it's silly, but I've never known how to throw overhand. I've always thrown underhand. So I said to myself, "By golly, I'm going to learn to do that. I'm going to have a respectable throw." I work at it, even to the point where it is not good for my shoulder.

I'm going out of town in a week, so I let my membership at the Health Club run out. And, gosh, I am really going to miss going to the Health Club. But I let my membership lapse because it was not worth it for me to buy a month's membership and then be gone for two weeks. That would be a scandalous thing for me to do. A friend of mine said, "Gosh, don't you think it would be worth it to treat yourself, to just go ahead and subscribe for the whole month, just because it means so much to you?" But I just can't treat myself with money. It doesn't work. Even the idea of treating myself feels meaningless. Because I know that I could have something if I wanted it, it is not like a treat. It is more like an extravagance, which feels bad.

The way I don't want to spend money on myself is miserly. I would much rather have the money safely in the bank, in some kind of long-term stock or something else that is safe, so that I can't just spend it on dinner or something. I hoard to the point where I get inconvenienced by it. I can't even enjoy myself in the way that I should be able to. I have a nice car, but I'm letting it fall to pieces. And I have a nice apartment, but it is filled with junky furniture. I don't want to spend money on things. If I can find something to make do, I will use that before I will go to a store and buy some new furniture. It all adds to a feeling of being lost and junky.

When I think of not having the money, I get terrified. It's a really undefined terror. I guess I'm afraid that I would just molder away in drudgery, like some character in a Russian novel. I also feel inadequate; I don't know if I could even do a job. I almost think that this very issue is something to be grateful for. I have the time to struggle with it, whereas I don't think I could experience my confusion if I was having to be consumed with the workaday world. But I am still waiting for that wonderful whatever-it-is I am saving myself for to come along. I wish I could just let the money give me opportunities. And gosh, I wish I could remove the greed and the fear that it won't be there, that there won't be enough, or that I'll be taken advantage of.

I'd like to know if there are people who can somehow deal with their money and who can have real relationships even though the money is there. I would also be interested in the difference between having money for money's sake, and money having some kind of liberating aspect that lets something more spiritual come out of it. If you have enough money, you should be free to open up and blossom, somehow, because you don't have to think so much about earning money, and maybe then you could give back to society or to the world or something in a different way. But I can't put my finger on it.

I guess my main wish would be just to let people who are reading this book know that other people are trying to deal with their money. If you can let go of some of the fear about money, then you don't have to feel the same desperation. Things might even work out okay.

# Homer Wallace

*Growing up in a formal household under the guidance of a perfectionist father, Homer Wallace has inherited a profound sense of responsibility along with his several million dollars. For him, the obligations that attend a family fortune seriously qualify the pleasures of wealth. In his mid-thirties, he is now wrestling with a question many young heirs ask themselves: how can I find my passion in life?*

I love having my wealth. It's very important to me; it's central to my personality in both good and bad ways. Interestingly, nobody else in my family appears to care as much about the family wealth and its future. My father may be gone tomorrow — he may get hit by a truck — and nobody in my family would be there to pick up. I'm not fooling myself that I could step up to replace him, but I have a huge financial interest in the company, and I enjoy the money. Prominent in my thoughts is what my father said when I was younger: If you don't cultivate your wealth, if you don't treat your wealth like the gem that it is, it will tarnish, it will disappear, it will leave you. And I don't want that to happen on my watch.

I have an interesting history on both sides of the family. Both my parents came from money. However, there are members of my extended family who don't have much money anymore because they spent their way out of their wealth. My mother's family is a fine example of that. My maternal grandfather was probably the wealthiest man in the state in the 1920s. My mother grew up with a dozen nannies. She was brought in to see her parents before dinner — very formal. A chauffeur took her to school in a limousine. And then the family lost most of its money during the Depression. My grandfather was a great man who was just devastated by what had happened. So all around me were examples of what could happen if I wasn't careful.

My great-grandfather Wallace founded a lumber company in the 1880s. That company was the source of much of my family's wealth. My grandfather was tight with his money and aggressively stern and, I think, fearful about the world and mindful of his obligations in a way that my other grandfather wasn't. So there are two distinct patterns in the two families. My father is a mercantilist, a capitalist. He's commercially driven, he loves business, he loves talking about money. My mother is more aesthetic, and she's bored with talk of money and business.

I always thought there was something extraordinary about my family's history. My name, Homer, is a family name, and it's a different kind of name. The house I grew up in is also unusual. So I was often aware that I was different from my friends.

My parents' house was designed by Philip Johnson, the famous architect who did the AT&T Building and the Seagram's Building in New York, and the glass house in New Canaan, Connecticut. So as you can well imagine if you have seen any of those buildings, the house is incredibly formal, and that formality certainly had its impact on me as a child. There is lots of glass and steel; the design is a little severe but also quite beautiful and balanced in its form. There are marble floors throughout, high ceilings, and a glass-enclosed garden that's probably thirty feet by thirty feet, with palm trees in it and a pond with fish. There is lots of contemporary art on the walls. We kids couldn't run around inside the house because it would be so easy to kick a ball through a window or damage a sculpture or a painting.

In front of the house was a large formal area paved with small stones that had to be raked every day. Alongside a very long driveway were about two hundred trees — perfectly spaced — one next to the other, all the way down. All those trees had to be watered and trimmed and fertilized, and of course that job fell on the shoulders of the kids. We were, in a way, a captive labor force in the Wallace kingdom. My father actually had the caretaker sculpt the snow banks to make ninety-degree angles straight up from the ground — I swear to God!

The maid seemed to know how to play her role according to my parents' preferences; she knew where to draw the line between formality and informality. She always wore a uniform, and when she had time off, she stayed in her wing of the house. She never owned a car; we gave her one of ours to use. It's almost as though my parents didn't want an old Chevy parked in the driveway.

Dinner at my house was a wonderful metaphor for a lot of other things about my family. My younger brother and I ate with Lorraine, the maid, in the kitchen until we had learned our table manners. We were allowed to join the rest of the family in the dining room when I was fourteen and he was twelve. The formality of our family was expressed in the way we talked to each other at the dinner table. That was where important discussions took place. Dinnertime was not an opportunity for the kids to have fun; we were expected to learn to communicate in an adult fashion and listen quietly to what my parents had to say.

My mother never cooked a meal in her life — certainly not while I was around. I was typically woken up by my mother, but breakfast was served by the maid. My bed was usually made while I was at breakfast, so that when I came back to my room, my school things were already set out for me. My mother drove us around and took us to hockey practice and things like that, but the maid was the one who cared for us. Lorraine played an important role in my upbringing, from the earliest days that I can recall until I was in college. There weren't too many kids who had that experience, and my friends certainly found out about "the help." They loved to come over and get Lorraine to make them chocolate shakes, and they used to call me just to hear her answer the phone. She'd say, "Waaallace residence." They'd laugh and hang up.

We were always given a lot of guidance on our behavior. [Laughs.] There was to be no foot dragging, whining, or spoiled behavior. I was pulled out of bed many times in the middle of the night because it was snowing, and I would have to go outside in six inches of snow to put covers over the garden beds. Papa wasn't about to hire someone to do those things, and for a long time, he didn't have a gardener. Instead, he got me out there with my brothers and sisters. I remember raking leaves after dark. My brother and I spent every day of our lives working around the house. We'd be picking the white stones out of the beige stones that were around the house and in the paths. Or we'd be pulling weeds in the orchard. Nothing on our property was out of line, and we were the ones who had to keep it that way. My father used say that there was nothing less than a hundred and ten percent. According to him, there was no reason to do anything unless you did it perfectly and precisely.

My friends didn't really want to come over to play because they would be put to work. I swear to God! It was labor camp — Stalag Wallace. To save a little time for play, we used to take my mother's Volvo station wagon and open the tailgate and put my friends in the back holding rakes. It was like a Zamboni on an ice rink. I would drive around the driveway, and we'd rake it that way.

That was my idea of fun, and it was about as much fun as it got at my house. I never had parties, and I rarely had girlfriends over. My mother was into her yoga, and I was afraid my father would say something weird, on top of how weird I already thought *I* was. I just didn't want to appear any more different. I felt very different from everyone because my name was Homer, I was tall and skinny, I had red hair, and I lived in a really bizarre house — in the Midwest! I so desperately wanted to be named Bob and be middle-sized with blonde hair and live in a normal house. I just wanted to be like everyone else.

I had mixed feelings about my father's formality. In some ways, I thought he was really uncool. Once he came to one of my soccer games, the last one of the season. My parents didn't usually come to school functions or athletic events. I remember him in his suit, standing away from the rest of the crowd, looking dapper and formal. He was a dashing man, but he wasn't like the rest of the fathers, who showed up in their khakis. And I was afraid that if I didn't do everything right, he would judge me in front of my friends. I was very fearful of my father. He was larger than life, he had a hell of a temper, and I didn't want to upset him.

Father wasn't around much to be fatherlike to me. Despite the fact that I've turned out rather normal as an adult, I think I suffered from the fact that my parents were gone a lot — often for weeks at a time. I feel that their wealth allowed them to be away so much. I needed their help to guide me. I rarely had my report card checked, and I never showed them my schoolwork — out of fear that they would either judge me or get angry over my grades.

58

I remember one time when my parents were in the Himalayas for a month. My older brothers and sisters were away at prep school and college, and my younger brother and I were the only ones at home. My parents had bought their Christmas gifts before they left and locked them in a guest bathroom. One day, my brother and I plotted to get into that bathroom. My brother went to distract the maid by asking her dumb questions about what was for dinner. Meantime, I got a screwdriver and unbolted the bathroom door from its hinges. We discovered that Mother gotten us a foosball game, which was what we had asked for. For days, we went on playing with that foosball game in the bathroom until we got bored with it. So when my mother came home, I said, "Mother, what I really want for Christmas is an air hockey game." My brother chimed in too, and my poor mother returned the foosball and got us the air hockey. We were so awful! I don't think there was a single Christmas that I didn't know exactly what I was getting. There were so many presents piled up under the Christmas tree that it was easy for me to disappear behind the boxes. I would use a razor blade to slit open all the packages that were for me and peek inside. It was pathetic.

Oftentimes my father talked to us kids about the responsibilities that came with having money. He talked about how money had played a big role in both families. He talked about the money as though it was something really special, but at the same time, he didn't want us to take it too seriously. So he tried to discount things so that they wouldn't have too much of an edge. On the way home in the car from Sunday dinner at the country club, he would say, in a way that was was rather indirect but also pointed, "There are a lot of directions we can take in life. It's really a shame that Uncle so-and-so or Aunt so-and-so has wasted their life by drinking." Or he would talk about how so-and-so never really worked, or how he developed an obsession for something or other — and how he lost all his money.

Without saying, "You kids are going to be a certain way, damn it, and this is the only way to do it," my father just kept on saying, "You have choices, and it really is up to you to get what you want out of life. Please think about it, and if you can, find some passion in life." And then he would lead into a conversation about money — how money grows, how easy it is to make money (that's what *he* thought!), but how nobody knows how to keep it. So the importance of money was instilled in my mind at a very young age. I remember Father saying that money is like a relationship: you need to learn how to love money in the same way as you need to learn how to love another person. Otherwise, he said, the money would disappear — you can't imagine how quickly it would disappear.

I remember how my father always used to talk about shirtsleeves to shirtsleeves in three generations. So as a teenager, I kept on wondering: am I the one who's going to lead the family back into the middle class?

It was my father's intention to give a lot of money to his kids at an early age for tax and estate planning purposes, so our money was always a part of our lives. He also believed that it offered us an opportunity at a young age to learn to handle money effectively. I started getting an income as a teenager, but I didn't dare touch it. A fair amount of my money was in trust, but I had at least a half a million free and clear. It wasn't as though the money was just sitting in my checking account, though. I would have had to make some phone calls and go by the gatekeeper with the magic word. But I was afraid to even talk to the gatekeeper — my father — about my money. It just wasn't part of my thinking that I would spend even a dime of it. Of course, that money has grown tremendously, so it was a good thing I didn't spend any.

My wealth had a huge impact on me when I was quite young. It was a handicap that has been hard to overcome. I was a millionaire at eighteen, and at times it was hard for me to sit down and memorize vocabulary for my high school English class when I knew that I had so much money I wouldn't ever have to work. Not that *not* working was an option, but it was hard for me to concentrate on something as banal as homework.

I was so distracted by thoughts of all that I could do that it was hard to choose what I wanted to do. I was always envious of my friends who knew what they wanted, especially the ones who wanted to go into medicine. I was an able student, but I never believed that I could concentrate enough in difficult science courses to become a doctor. That belief was balanced with foolish thoughts like, "I don't want to be a doctor. Anyone can be a doctor." To me, being a professional seemed like a step backward in a perverse kind of way. I was going to be a man of the world and have a really interesting life, as opposed to just some professional existence.

There also were moments when I thought, "I've been given this gift by God, and it's really quite special. I should be out saving people, doing something in Africa, or a mile from here, where people really need help."

I also wanted my father to be proud of me; I wanted to prove that despite all I had been given, I could make it in business. So I decided to go to business school because I thought it would teach me skills that would give me lots of choices. My decision was balanced with thinking that I should have learned things that didn't leave me with so many choices, but which resulted in deeper understanding and more effectiveness. The bottom line, no doubt, was that I hoped that by following the kinds of interests my father had, he would appreciate me and love me more.

I sometimes feel like I'm waiting in the wings for my father to die, so that I can step into a position of responsibility in the family business. But if I worked for him now, it would be a battle. I'd be trying to prove myself to him and somehow maybe diminish him or eclipse him, which would be hard for him to handle. And I know that he would do that to me. He'd get very frustrated and snappy with me, and I think that we would try to crush each other in the process. I think that's what happened between my father and his own father.

I often feel as though I'm the only one in our family who will be able to take care of the family's wealth, the family business. From a young age, I have known that I didn't want to end up as a naive rich boy who didn't know how to deal with financial professionals. I've seen that kind of thing happening with some of my extended family. I've seen a lot of my aunts and uncles and cousins interact with money managers in a really dysfunctional manner. My relatives were so perverse about the whole thing: They thought that the world was out to rip them off, that the professionals didn't have their best interests in mind. Working with money managers is like being in a personal relationship, but some of my relatives haven't known how to treat these people like partners; they've treated them like hired help. And many have seen one professional manager after another leave unhappy. Some of my relatives have seen their wealth diminish, but I'll never let that happen. The family money is a huge responsibility, and in some ways it's a burden.

I want people to think, "Gee, Homer Wallace is really a together guy. Despite all the stuff that could have screwed him up, he has it together." But some of that appearance of being together is an illusion. I'm thirty-three years old, and I still haven't gotten my career to a level where I can support myself in the house I live in. I'm pretty hard on myself, and I haven't really figured out what my joy in life is. I want to have more fun and not be so serious. And my fear is that some day, someone's going to say, "He was such a nice, charming guy, but he's kind of a failure. He's one of those fourth-generation kind of guys who act responsibly and do all of the things expected of a rich person. He had a lot of passion, but he didn't go down his path of joy." That's my big fear, and that's what I'm contending with right now.

# Fred Hopgood

*Love, commitment, vulnerability, and money are all twisted together in Fred Hopgood's experience. His adolescent battles with his father are the emotional backdrop for his current struggles with his wealth. As his marriage was falling apart, he began to see that his ambivalence toward money had become enmeshed with his feelings for his wife. He now believes his wealth has held him back from making serious commitments. Hopgood longs to get beyond the tether of his inheritance and connect himself more deeply to others.*

I t's true that you can uncover things if you start talking about them. I've never talked about this money stuff before — ever. When I talk about it, I start to relax: I see that it isn't such a big deal. Maybe it is all in my mind, and I can work with it. I've been giving myself a headache for so long, but maybe it's just not that big a deal.

My great-grandfather and his brothers were farmers who cashed in on the big lumber boom in Wisconsin in the nineteenth century. They built warehouses for the lumber that was coming down the Mississippi, and then they bought property in northern Wisconsin and started to lumber themselves. It was actually the story of the Great American Dream: they had an idea, and it grew and grew and grew. My grandfather was a powerful man. He consolidated the business in Milwaukee, he was running operations in Georgia, Washington, and British Columbia, and he didn't lose the business during the Depression. He was a sergeant in World War I, and he brought up his kids in a military fashion. They had to follow strict rules; it was like boot camp. My father was expected to work for the family business after college, and he did — although he wanted to go to graduate school and study history.

Both my grandparents were legendary, magical people to us grandchildren, and their wealth was really obvious to us. They lived in a big, white mansion — beautiful and simple, with a huge grand staircase. My grandmother was powerful, magnetizing, beautiful, elegant — amazing! Grandfather was somewhat awesome. He was his own guy, and he influenced all of us to be our own guys, too.

My parents moved out to the country to get some breathing space from my grandparents' world. They built a ranch-style modern house on three hundred acres of farmland, and they became a 1950s suburban American couple, like the Cleavers in "Leave it to Beaver." That was the world I grew up in, and I loved it.

The area where we lived ended up being populated by rich people. Our nearest neighbors were much richer and more flaunty than we were, so we thought we were absolutely normal. We didn't know we were rich. Most of the families we knew had the same things. Everybody had boats, and everybody had ski-doos. The poor people were so *away* that we didn't see them. They were just the poor people, but everyone else was the same as us. And everybody else was everybody. We thought we were middle class — not even upper-middle class.

It wasn't until I started to have an outer world — like the Buddha, who went outside the walls of his palace and for the first time saw old people and sick people — that I suddenly realized that the majority of people were suffering a lot worse than me. That was shocking. I didn't know! That was where things were covered up in my family. My parents had been protecting us from that knowledge, and protecting themselves, too. I started to understand something because of the hush-hush whenever we drove through a poor neighborhood; my parents never said anything then.

At first my father tried to emulate his father's military style of bringing up children, but he wasn't too successful. I had the easiest time of any of the kids because I was the next-to-youngest of four, and my father's rigidity was gradually breaking down.

I went to the best private school in Saint Louis. That school had strong traces of the English school system, but they were being obliterated by the time I got there. And I spent a lot of time at the country club. I had tennis lessons, golf lessons, and swimming lessons. In the winter I went to the club every day and played hockey. The country club was a magical place for me. It was where I started to be aware of girls; it was where I went to dances.

At home, we had cows and horses and cats and dogs. I had to feed the cows. We had our own pool, and we swam all summer. The neighbors used to come over to use the pool, and our house was a hive of activity. I had a happy childhood.

My happy life started to fall apart when I was about fourteen. My parents were getting really heavy with me in terms of work. They wanted me to start growing up, but I didn't want to grow up; I was having too much fun. I had decided that I was going to do my own thing, and my father had no influence on me. Things got really bad between us.

My parents took me to a psychiatrist when I was seventeen or eighteen. He was on my side, and they were really pissed off about that. I was getting a heavy message from my parents that I was fucked up, and I was trying to say, over and over, that I wasn't fucked up. I had a vision, and I thought I was doing the right thing. But my parents were saying, "You're not doing the right thing because you're not working. You're not doing this, you're not doing that, you're just rebelling." The writing and art I was doing were probably incredibly self-indulgent, but other people liked them, and they encouraged me.

I became a rebel at school. I was put on probation, and I didn't go back to school for my senior year. I had started smoking pot in seventh or eighth grade. In fact, all the richest guys in my class became dopeheads early on. I was into the whole Incredible String Band, folksy, Donovan scene. I played my mandolin and tried to grow my hair as long as my father would let me.

My father was mad at me, and I was snotty to him. So I moved out of my parents' house and got my own place — just a little garret. I wrote plays. I was taking on the guise of being poor. My friends were all becoming alcoholics and drug users, but I never did anything that bad. I did sort of irritating things, like getting amazingly drunk at the country club with two friends and careening around the golf course in a cart, like the three stooges, digging holes in the greens. That was one of the last awful things I ever did to my father. It wasn't that I hated my parents. I still loved them, but I was a teenager — confused about love, hate, and hypocrisy. I called my parents hypocrites.

65

They wouldn't kick me out; they were afraid I might become a drug addict or something. They gave me money to get an apartment, so I didn't have to work. And I think my father really regrets doing that. My parents thought that if they gave me a long leash, I'd come around and become an architect. They thought I was going to change any minute. And to this day, I don't think things have changed a whole great deal. I think there's an aspect of umbilicalness to the money that has had a profound influence on my actions.

I decided to become a vegetarian, and I gave up drinking and smoking. I was romantic, and I was attracted to mysticism. There was a swami in town, and I went and saw a Zen master, but I don't remember which one. Then I went to college for a year, but I never finished college. I was too restless.

Then I decided to leave Saint Louis and go to New York. My parents were nervous about me taking off for New York. Dad said, "How much money will you need?" and I said, "What about maybe $300 a month?" I had no idea how much I could ask for, and I didn't feel I had any right to the money. I was not willing to work — no matter what, and my father would have had to cut me off in order to make me work, but he never did. So I just existed on what he was willing to give me. Three hundred bucks in New York would run out in two weeks. I remember walking past Balducci's in Greenwich Village and drooling, but I didn't have a cent. I'd just spent my last money on two bunches of asparagus, and that would be my dinner in my cold loft.

I was mugged twice. Once I had just gotten my $300, and the money was in my wallet. I had gotten drunk at a jazz club, and at two in the morning I walked out on the street, and someone rammed me against the wall, pulled out my wallet and ran away. My entire allowance was taken from me! So I told my parents that I'd been robbed, and they sent me more money.

I became a lonely refugee — away from the family. I was obsessed with fame, but I didn't work hard on my art; I didn't know how to work. If I had had to make money at that point, I would have become something. I used to spend money on other people. My friends were a pack of poor, starving artists; I was the only one who came from money. I'd pay for my friends' drinks and stuff like that. And I had friends who used to tell me I shouldn't be doing that.

I never asked my parents how much money I had. And I didn't *want* to know. I was having a major battle with my father, so how was I going to ask him? I couldn't say, "Okay, I hate you. Now just gimme my money." I was kept umbilically attached to my father, even though I totally disagreed with everything he said.

I was afraid to ask for more money, and I was guilty about how I was spending the little bit I had. Then gradually I started to call the family office and ask for more money. I'd call up and talk to the secretary. I didn't talk to my dad about money any longer, and he didn't want to have anything to do with it. There were many years in my life when I could have been doing things, but because I had this ignorant fogginess about my money, I didn't do them.

I actually believed that I was somewhat poor. For years, I never really bought anything. Once I bought a car. It was my first major purchase. I didn't look for a Porsche or anything; I got a used Ford Fairmont station wagon. It was great, but it wasn't expensive at all. I don't even remember what I paid — maybe $7,000 or $8,000. I didn't have any sense of proportion as to how much was available to me.

I still don't have the foggiest idea how much money I have. I think it's because I don't want to know so that I won't have to worry about spending it. I'm paranoid about spending too much. Nobody at the family office has been calling me up and telling me that I should stop spending money, although that did happen for a few years. Maybe it's time for me to . . . I mean, I know approximately what I have: It's got to be above a million dollars — right?

After I got married, I got a lot of hell from my wife because I didn't know how to buy a house, I didn't know how to buy furniture, I didn't know how to buy curtains — so I hesitated. Every step of the way, I hesitated, and I felt weird. And then I started to question whether I loved her or not. So the money issues merged right into our relationship, and it all became a total hassle. We had a joint bank account, but she couldn't just go and spend the money. She was not really acknowledged as a joint owner until we got divorced, and then she automatically became heiress to a ton of money. It was like the Mafia: the people at the family office basically said, "How much do we have to give her to just go away?"

I have always caught a lot of hell from the women in my life because they know I'm rich, and they think I don't spend enough money on them. They say that I don't love them. Maybe I need to put some money into my relationship to make my girlfriend feel better, or something. So what should I do about that? Should I go and buy her something to make her feel better?

The whole thing of being taken advantage of has been coming up for me. One of the things that drove my ex-wife crazy was that people were always dropping in to hang out and drink. That's always been part of my life with money. A bunch of guys expected that they could come over any time and pour tons of alcohol down their throats. Then I'd have to shuffle them out. It was completely humiliating. And I was drinking too much and spending too much.

Recently I confronted one of my friends about the way I thought he was using me — sucking up my liquor — and he said he understood. But he's still doing it. It hurts me in a place that I've been hurt before. I know that I may be overdoing it, and my friends don't mean any harm. But it's an ongoing process of my being generous and open, and then there is a moment when I can see that they are not doing it *with* me; they are doing it by themselves, and they are using me. It's incredibly humiliating.

I'm at a point where nothing has really changed; I am still the same as I was when I left home. I feel like I need a counselor — somebody who could make suggestions and not put me down for being uptight, somebody who could sympathize with my confusion over how to extend my wealth to myself and to others. I am going to be forty, and I don't know what I'm good at. I seem to be a little bit good at a few things, and I've done a little bit of everything — lithography, silk screen, theater, writing, film. But I never focused. And I've never spent much money on my art or on myself. I've spent money on a house or on a car, but I haven't spent it to publish my own work. I could have bought a computer system which would print out something like a book, but I haven't done it. I just don't know how to go about fulfilling my dreams, so I don't do anything. I don't know how to connect with the world. I keep wondering if having money is actually holding me back from communicating with the world.

# Raleigh Jordan

*Raleigh Jordan's childhood world was defined by superlatives — the richest father in Baltimore, the finest lessons with the best teachers, the most exquisite showcase home. From her lush environment, she derived a feeling of endless safety, a sense that she was protected from all the dangers of life. Her bubble burst when her husband lost her entire inheritance playing the stock market. Raised in the days when women unquestioningly turned over their financial affairs to their husbands, Jordan experienced a disillusionment and loss that may strike a familiar chord with other wealthy women.*

Wherever I have gone, I have been quite aware, quite aware of being wealthy, having always been wealthy, having always had money, never having had to worry. I'm very conscious of it, and it causes me to feel guarded, not in the sense of not letting anyone know because they might take some of it, but guarded almost in a confusion of embarrassment or apology. It isn't shame, it's a sense of, "Uh oh, if this gets out, I'll have to apologize."

The experience has been almost like bumping your nose on something you thought was clear space, but it's glass that is so clean you can't see it. You have to stop and pull back, and there's a reassessment going on all the time. It's a fine line. You feel guilty, but then immediately you draw back, and you know that guilt isn't the correct reaction. It's a mixture of guilt, apology, and separateness. It's part of a syndrome which still exists in me, although not to the point where I'm going to self-destruct or be foolish. I have had this syndrome since I was very, very young because obviously I was aware very early of being different.

As a child of three or four, I developed the belief that if I gave my things away, I wouldn't have to apologize. I became a giver. "Here, take it. Take my doll. I've got five of them. Take one." I placated because of a fear that I'd be shunned, or people would think less of me. So I'd even it out. What people do, I discovered with the man I later married, is they attribute to you, who are wealthy, attitudes you don't have, but which they imagine they would have if *they* were wealthy. So they plaster this all over you, and then they say, "Well, of course, you're stuck up because . . . ," or "You feel as if you're better because . . ." So as a child I'd level the playing field, and I would do it by distributing my possessions, in an even-handed fashion, before you would even ask. I wouldn't even let you get to the point of asking. Then you would like me.

I remember being five and going to play with a girl who was older. I was a little intimidated. She was eight years old, a grown woman, and I was only five. Without asking, she took my child's set of exquisite, old, Willow-pattern china, and claimed that I had given it to her. And this I didn't do. It was an entire set with three serving platters — the largest, the medium, the small — and vegetable dishes with covers, and dinner plates, and the underliners in two sizes, and cups and saucers. She also took a complete miniature set of sterling silver, including iced-tea and iced-coffee spoons. The way she took them was, she said to me, "Come over to my house and bring your china and your silver. We'll play dolls." Well, that sounds delicious to a five-year-old. I was honored. I damn near broke all my fingers off my hands getting it together to go. I was going to have a wonderful afternoon. At one point, I went out of her playroom, and when I came back and said, "I have to go now. My daddy's picking me up, and I want to get my things together," in that short period of time, my china and silver spoons were gone. And she said, in high dudgeon, "But you gave them to me! You gave me the dishes. You gave me the silver. Don't you remember?" And she became utterly irate and furious. I have never been quite so hysterical.

That was my first introduction to hysteria and to theft and to human nature and to all of what it later led to, but I was too young to figure it out. And that's where it started. Believe it or not, this has become a syndrome in my life — people taking from me and then claiming that I indicated they could: "You owe it to me because you have so much."

When I was born in 1936, my father was, no question, the wealthiest man in Baltimore. Everybody knew it. He was director of this, that, and the other. So everybody was aware of who he was and who I was. It seems to me that I always, always knew. The wealth was all wrapped up in my father. And from the beginning there was never a doubt about who he was. He was an immense man, tall and barrel-chested. He was a figure of importance. And he was so wonderfully electric and magnetic and alive and warm and welcoming and hugging and approachable.

My father made his fortune very, very early. He had his own company by the time he was, I think, sixteen. He had board and paper factories and box factories. He made both rough boxes and exquisite fine boxes, like ladies' dress boxes. He had already made a lot of money long, long before I was ever born. He made a huge fortune during the war years because paper board and anything for packaging were in demand. He also invested in the stock market, and he bought gold futures and commodities. He was very shrewd. Investing is what he did at night. During the day, he ran his factories, and at night, he spent from after dinner until eleven o'clock with the *Wall Street Journal*.

You've got to realize what my surroundings were. They were the finest of ev-e-ry-thing. For example, my father went and bought out the W.S. Sloan estate in New York. He was an aficionado of Oriental rugs and Oriental ceramics and china, and these things were all over the house. I'll tell you what it was like. Remember the movie, four or five years ago, with Cheryl Ladd playing Barbara Hutton, *The Barbara Hutton Story*? Burl Ives played F.W. Woolworth, her grandfather. My youngest daughter was in college when she saw that movie, and she called me up and said, "Mom, this is you. This was your life, except that you were smarter."

My surroundings, you see, were truly palatial. The house was a stone Tudor mansion with three-foot thick walls. The man who built it had emptied out a quarry to make that house. In the dining room, there was a Czechoslovakian crystal chandelier to end all chandeliers. About every three months was chandelier-cleaning day. I can remember the German maids with their hair covered in huge white caps, like shower caps. They'd put a small table under the chandelier and stand on it and unhook each crystal, one by one, and wash it in the water. The English butler would be standing there, and they'd hand a crystal to him, and he would dry it and hand it back to the girls, and they'd hang it back up and go to the next one. It took them all day long. I don't know why, when my mother sold that house in 1973, she sold the chandelier along with the house. Even my children were heartbroken.

Each piece of furniture had its place. My father had George Pothast — the premier German cabinet maker from a whole family tradition of cabinet makers going back to the sixteenth century — come up to New York with him on his private railroad car. Father took him to the furniture wing of the Metropolitan Museum of Art and pointed out which pieces of furniture he wanted George to copy exactly, right down to each piece of inlay, and George Pothast did it. I was aware of the exquisite importance of each item. This wasn't just a dining table, this wasn't just a sideboard, this wasn't just a mirror. These weren't just black-and-white squares under your feet. This was Carrara marble, and I knew where it came from and how it was cut. There was a gold-rimmed mirror above a huge mantelpiece over the fireplace in the dining room. The rooms in that house had ten- or twelve-foot ceilings, and that mirror went from flush with the mantel all the way up to the ceiling. And it was framed with thick, heavy, real gold. There was a pool table that was handmade for Daddy with pearls and mother-of-pearl and ivory studs around the edges. He taught me how to play pool when I was so young that I had to stand on a footstool. Everywhere there was such overwhelming opulence and comfort and quality — especially quality. I was aware of the limitless array and extent of quality.

You could go from room to room, and you'd move into this gigantic fifty-foot living room, and beyond that, you moved into the sun parlor that had a huge pool, all made of fieldstone, filled with prize carp raised by a man up in western Pennsylvania. The carp were a foot long, and they were swimming around. We had a person who was responsible for taking care of the carp. He had to make sure the pH level in the water was correct, and he had to make sure the carp were being fed the proper thing.

And then you walked from there out into the azalea walkway and the rose gardens. That was where I had my wedding reception, in that azalea pathway. People came from the church, and all the limos were lined up in the front of the house. The garden was delicious! Mmm.

You'd hear the lawnmower starting up, and then you could smell the cut grass smell come floating up, and the smell of honeysuckles. There were beds and beds of honeysuckles and lilies of the valley, and I'd run out and pick them all and smell them. And we had these fountains these different places you could go. It was like a park.

Everywhere there was a lot of detail, and there was a lot of care. I had a sense of appreciating each item for itself and the place it was meant to be in. There was a sense of order, which is very important. Order. There was nothing disordered, let alone disorderly. Everything that was done was appropriate. Dress was appropriate. There was a sense of fineness.

Dinner was six o'clock sharp. Not at 5:50, not at 6:05 — at six. And it was extremely, extremely formal. We had an English butler and two maids. The maids wore formal maids' uniforms. They wore black at night with the white apron and the white cap, and during the day, they wore light blue with the white apron and a different kind of a cap. At night, the cap was conical, pointing up. And during the day, it was a smaller cap. I would sit at this gigantic table, and my mother and my father would sit at the ends. That table must have been twenty-four feet long.

I never saw my father without his tie, except very late at night. I'd peek in and say "Goodnight, Daddy," and I'd see him in a bathrobe, but that was upstairs. Never did I see either one of my parents, outside of their own separate boudoirs, when they weren't completely dressed up.

They each had their separate everything — separate bedrooms, sitting rooms, bathrooms. And I had my own separate quarters, too, with exactly the same layout. And of course, Daddy had his own private railroad car. Every two weeks we'd go down to the B & O station, and they'd hook up his railroad car, and we'd go to New York, the three of us. In those days, the black people were the stewards. I was born in '36, so it was around '42. Father had a suite at the Commodore Hotel. The Commodore was like another home to me. Father always had those trips planned ahead. He'd have front-row tickets for all the shows on Broadway. I'd seen Helen Hayes by the time I was three. It was the last of the old times.

In the summers, we'd go to the ____ Club in New York State for four months. It was extremely exclusive in those days. You could hardly be an Italian, and you certainly couldn't be black, and you certainly could not be Jewish. I tell you, there was an exclusivity about it. One of my father's attorneys was Jewish, and my father had a lot of legal work to get done, so this attorney was flown up in a company aircraft. The only way this Jewish lawyer was permitted to set foot on the grounds of the ____ Club was to arrive at night. He had to hang around somewhere else until it got dark, and then they had to sneak him in by the servants' entrance. And in their generosity, the board of directors allowed him to stay overnight in a two-foot by four-foot room the size of a closet in the servants' quarters.

I had the best lessons for everything. We had a Steinway, and I had a harmony teacher from the Peabody School of Music who came twice a week for an hour. One lesson was theory and one was harmony. This was very high level. It wasn't just piano lessons: I already had the piano lessons with Mrs. Gaminder, who was my German piano teacher. And I had an Olympic gold medalist as my swimming instructor at the Greenbrier down in West Virginia. And when we'd go to the Broadmoor in Colorado Springs, I had a skating instructor there. And I had riding lessons up at the ____ Club and in Baltimore. When I think about it now, it was totally ideal and breathtaking.

As soon as the war was over, we'd go to Europe on the *Queen Mary* or the *Queen Elizabeth*, and I'm talking about Q.E. One! And then, of course, the great thing later on, in the fifties, was the *Ile de France*. I would take all my final exams for high school a month early. I was the valedictorian anyway, so it didn't matter. And you had the servants helping and running around and ironing things and getting ready to pack the big steamer trunks. Each of us had our own trunks inscribed with our names and addresses. Everything was personalized. And when we'd go up the gangplank, we always had the center suite on the main deck. Daddy always explained everything to me: why we had that suite on the *Queen Mary* or the *Queen Elizabeth* or the *Ile de France*. It was because you didn't get the roll, the pitch, that you got on the ends. He could afford the very best, and we always had the very best. It was that simple.

We had our Swiss chauffeur from Génève, whose name was Marcel Tinglis, waiting for us at Southampton. I went to the coronation of Queen Elizabeth. It was all of an era. But that era is gone by now, and it cannot be recreated. It was the end of the era of the *Titanic* and the

Astors. Being on those ocean liners was like being on a movie set to show what life was like on the *Titanic*. Thank heavens I missed that trip!

And when you go to Paris, you don't go scrounging around with a guidebook in your hand, because Marcel the chauffeur was there at Cherbourg or Le Havre with a black stretch limo. And you'd go to the Tour D'Argent, and you'd go to Maxim's. Whatever it was, it was always, always, always the best. So when other boys and girls were working through the summer as lifeguards or in Woolworths or something, I was on the *Queen Mary* or I was up at the _____ Club.

Now what was my attitude about all this? First of all, you aren't born into two lives so that you can compare. You live one life. You're born into one environment, unless that changes dramatically, which mine did not, of course. There was nothing like my world for stability. It was stable, it was predictable in the good sense, and it was non-boring. There are plenty of people who would have turned out spoiled and lazy if they had been born into a situation like that. But I was not spoiled.

My mother's family were highly cultured people, and they were industrious and smart and businesslike. My great-grandfather accumulated a fortune, but my mother's father lost his wife's fortune. So that particular scenario skipped a generation. My grandfather did to my grandmother exactly what my husband later did to me. My grandmother was well known as the most eligible German heiress in Baltimore, but she married a rolling stone. My grandfather's father was the aide-de-camp of Kaiser Wilhelm, but my grandfather was a black sheep, a womanizer, a bad seed — no question.

All the "shoulds" and the "should nots" and the "I don't approves" came from my mother. The messages I received from her really didn't have to do with money, they had to do with her mental constructs, her Christian Science. My mother was the fly in the ointment; she was the nest full of hornets at the wedding party. She was raining on the parade that I had with my father. She was somebody I had to get around, to placate, and to avoid if possible. One day, my mother put me in her Auburn, and I was so little that my little white socks and little white Mary Janes just hit the edge of the seat. And she drove me down to the, quote, "colored" section in Baltimore. There were row houses, which Baltimore is famous for, and the black people were out sitting on the steps and milling around and hanging out of windows. And my mother took quite a while driving around there. She said, "I just wanted you to see that not everybody lives the way you do." But it wasn't a surprise for me because I'd been travelling exactly the same route, going to Daddy's offices with him. So she thought she was showing me something new, but my attitude was: I know this already. I hate to get too esoteric, but I honestly am a very evolved soul, and I already knew about poverty.

I remember the day, when I was thirteen, that my father bought me my first car. "I have something to show you," he said, and we got into his Cadillac Fleetwood. (He changed it every year or two.) We went to this showroom, and here's this robin's-egg blue Buick convertible revolving very slowly on a turntable. It had black leather seats. Oh! I flipped. I fell in love with it, and I danced around and said, "Oh, it's so beautiful!" And Daddy walked over to the manager, had a word with him, and came back with the keys in his hand. And on the key chain was a miniature of the license plate. He handed the keys to me and said, "It's yours." After that, I went everywhere. I drove to New York, I drove to Washington, I drove to Atlantic City. Now I know you're thinking, "You must have been spoiled rotten, and to an idiotic degree." But I wasn't spoiled. Not spoiled. Daddy was very strict about money.

Everything in my childhood world was specific, everything had its place. There was order, order within opulence. It wasn't overdone. There was nothing overdone. It was just exquisite, and everything was of the best. Now the feeling that I always had, right from the beginning, was one of total security, total protection. Endless! "This will never change." When I think about what I have since learned, what has happened, it was an incredible sense of safety and protection. And the hidden message I had from my father was [whispering]: "It'll never change. This is for always! This is the world. It will always be there." The assurance was that those were things I didn't ever have to worry about. Now a child doesn't say, "I wonder if it'll always be there if you aren't here any more." A child doesn't do that because she's eternal.

When I was in college, I met a fellow from a wealthy family in San Diego, and he took a great shine to me. He invited me out for a prom at Stanford, so I flew out for the weekend. Today it wouldn't be such a big thing, but it was a big deal in '54. Sometime after that was Sophomore Fathers' Day at my college, and my father was there. I can see it now. It was at dinner, and the subject between the fathers got to be, "You know, there are some very, very wealthy girls here." Daddy was just sitting there listening. All of a sudden, the father who brought up the whole subject said, "I heard that just a few weeks ago there was a girl from here who flew all the way out to Stanford for a weekend." I was on my chicken fricasee and peas, and my father said, "Really?" And the other father said, "Yeah, I understand that her father just wrote a check and she went." I guess that's how people saw me. To them, I was a rich girl, and all that those words imply.

*Raleigh Jordan married Frank Morrison when she was in graduate school at Harvard. She married him because he wanted to marry her and because she was pregnant and did not know what else she could do.*

A day or two before I married this guy Frank, I was sitting in an obstetrician's office, and I read a statistic in a magazine about the odds of men who are not wealthy or from the upper classes marrying heiresses. This was May, 1959. The chance of being a poor boy with no assets and no background marrying a wealthy heiress was one in fourteen million. It was as if Cassandra and the whole Greek chorus were chanting to me, "Beware! Beware!"

I didn't like Frank. Marrying him was an act of nobility. I realized what I had done the day of the wedding. This was a guy who dropped the facade. Asshole! He dropped the facade! I don't think it works for a man or a woman who has inherited money to marry, quote, "beneath his (or her) station." I'm not disparaging persons from, quote, "a lower social stratum." I'm not looking down upon them, but it's like oil and water. It's the whole environment, the ambiance, the habits, the speech patterns, the expectations, the regularity. There's something that comes with solid, settled wealth. Never mind that my father was the one who made it; it wasn't like "new" money. Let's remember that he made it forty years before I was born. This was settled wealth. Daddy didn't win the Irish sweepstakes. We were different from working-class households, where people throw mashed potatoes at each other.

Frank's father died tragically when he was five years old, and they were from almost poverty. He was a *poseur*. He somehow managed to turn himself out so that he appeared to be something he's not. Doesn't this remind you of a classic English novel? He got shot into the stratosphere with my money. He got dizzy with that kind of rapid rise in his fortunes. When he walked down the church aisle and married me, it was exactly as if he'd won the lottery. And do you know what happens to people who suddenly give up their $300-a-week plumbing job because they won the lottery? They cannot handle it on any level. The top level of society probably have vicious mouths behind closed doors, but people who are on a lower socio-economic level vent their frustrations in the only way available to them, which is free. It's called the fishwife syndrome, and this is what he was raised with. This is how you deal with things.

It was back to the tea set for me: Frank came to expect that I would rescue him time and again. He went from that scratching-around, can-we-have-chicken-at-the-end-of-the-week? poverty to having everything that my wealth implied. It wasn't just the money. He also moved into the way of life I had always known — the exotic trips, for instance. I literally made it possible for this man to see the world, and always first class. We spent weeks touring Peru and Mexico. We took a month-long safari through Kenya, Tanzania, and Uganda at a cost of over $21,000. We toured the Portugese Algarve, we cruised the Mediterranean, and we went on a grand tour of Turkey and Greece. Of course, there were also many elegant trips all over Europe. Frank even treated himself to a hugely expensive fishing trip north of the Arctic circle.

Frank was getting drunk on my wine, all right. He bought himself a $100,000 vintage Lamborghini Muira. He also had a Lamborghini Espada, a Ferrari, one or two Corvettes, and a Mercedes gull-wing coupe — all bought with my money. I vividly recall the day he phoned me from his brokerage office to anounce his decision to acquire the Muira. "I think I owe it to myself to have a Muira," he declared. Me? — I always had a Chrysler station wagon because in addition to everything else I had thirteen Great Danes.

I'm trying to explain how it happened, how I married this guy, and how he was able to lose my fortune. The major error was that my father was elderly and failing, and he died three years after I married. It was at that moment that my husband finally revealed his true colors. There should have been precautions. You have this slick con artist, this Robert Preston Music Man that I married, and nobody saw through him. It's a very risky proposition to be of wealth, of an inherited, solid, luxurious, stable wealth background, whether male or female, but mostly female, and to marry someone without any money of his own. You create an enormous gap, an enormous discrepancy! You're going to have problems with resentment, like I did. He's going to resent you. He's going to do extra special foolish, stupid things in order to try to, quote, "measure up." Or he'll want to make his own bundle just to show you that he could do what your father did. All this was part of it. Somebody is going to suffer from it, and I certainly did. There should have been a surveillance set up, and the minute the surveillance showed what this character was doing, the money should have been taken out of his hands and given to a professional money manager.

My father died in 1962, and it took four years to probate his will. He gave half of his private assets to Mother and half to me. Mother and I got twenty per cent each of his companies. His sons from his first two marriages got the rest of the companies. My share amounted to $4 million. I was not the wealthiest person in the world, although I had more money than Patty Hearst ever did even when they kidnapped her. This is what makes me so angry and hurts so much in retrospect. Frank, a totally worthless, undeserving entity, a person who never had any history with my father, actually became, in effect, the heir to my fortune. I never saw or handled the money. The funds were transferred by Daddy's friend, a judge in Baltimore, directly up to Frank's brokerage office in Boston. For all intents and purposes, Frank took control of it.

The only income he ever made was churning my account. He had token clients to make him look like he was actually working. Why should he work? Why do it? It's like the plumber who quits his job the minute he finds out he has won the lottery. Why should he go and, quote, "bust his ass," in his language? Why? When he's got all that money? And my attitude was: there is so much money, who cares?

I had a lot of money, so it wasn't like I was going to go live in a hovel. The first thing I did was to find an estate. I found one — on eighty acres of rolling countryside, built in 1929, when everybody was jumping out of windows in New York. It was the showplace of showplaces. So I bought it, and I intended to live there forever and ever. I created that place. It wasn't a house, it was a way of life. It was called Juniper Rock, and it had everything — I don't even know how many rooms — and I had it redone. It had a formal English garden with an Italian stone wall at one end, and a fountain shaped like a shell with a figurine and water dripping into the shell. You'd think you were in the Gardens of Tivoli outside Rome. I had them take down part of that wall and put in the most luxurious swimming pool, and I built a cabana with a perky yellow and white striped flag on top.That cabana was fully equipped with counters and a refrigerator and an icemaker and a changing room. I did all that. And then I revamped the house, modernized it, this exquisite country estate. And when you stood there looking out, you could swear that you were looking at some *paysage* from Alfred de Musset. You'd look out, and it was rolling and wispy and so romantic. There was a road curving over a bridge and a trout pond and junipers and cypresses cascading down a hill. And there was a coach house with an eight-car garage and stables underneath. It was just exquisite. I put a lot of my heart and soul into that estate. It was like a Camelot. I identified with the place; it was me. And I lost that place after Frank squandered my fortune. That's why I'm so crushed now because I put a lot of heart into everything. The only visible, palpable payoff, so far, is my children. That is a discernible asset that comes directly from the heart, the soul, the attention to detail.

I was very much on the social circuit in those years. Part of it was to get back at Frank. I was bored out of my skull with this man. I was having one to two hundred people in for big, huge parties every two months. I had these braziers lighting the way. Once I had a huge party with tents, and we had two or three hundred people. I built the dance floor, I had the orchestra, I had the round tables. I designed all of the tablecloths — multicolored with gold fringes. One guy ended up asleep in the pachysandra. I created a momentum because there wasn't any in the marriage. And all this time, of course, I was floating on the same ocean of plenty that I had grown up with and had all my life.

In 1966, I already had four children and was about to have a fifth. Try to picture it. The money had a lot to do with it; a person in poverty wouldn't do this. She'd be too shocked. If you were in poverty, if you didn't have independent means, you would not say, "I will now have one child after the next after the next after the next." So as you can imagine, I was busy with all those children, and I didn't know what Frank was doing at the office. I never signed the money over to him, I never wrote down a thing saying, "Half is yours, half is mine," or "All of it is yours." I didn't sign anything. The money was in my name. You know how he manipulated me? He'd bring a blank stock pad home, and sure enough, when I was fooling around feeding the kids breakfast, with the orange juice and scrambled eggs and toast, and a car pool was coming, that's when he'd put this stock pad down in front of me on the kitchen table and say, out of the side of his mouth, "You gotta sign these 'cause I gotta get moving now." He puts the pad down in front of me, and I'm fooling with the children, and I'm writing my name, I'm signing my money away.

By '71, I'll bet he had lost half of my inheritance, and by the end of '72 or '73, I think he had lost it all. He was floating on thin air, and I was doing it to myself by signing my name to those stock powers. He was shrewd and calculating. He didn't come around with his stock powers when I had nothing else to do and would have had time to focus. When I hear myself saying this, it sounds pretty damn stupid. What was I doing? All I can say is that I had made assumptions about Frank's intelligence when I suddenly realized, Whoah! Wait a minute. It simply didn't occur to me that anybody could lose that kind of money. I didn't have a clue that it was all collapsing until it was over.

At the end, I had $5,000 to my name, and an estate that cost, in those days, five, six, seven thousand dollars a month to run. And what made me so angry is that it took my father from age sixteen until he died at age eighty-one to accumulate that kind of money. And the stories that Daddy used to tell me about what he'd done in the old days in New York when he was sixteen to save a nickel or a dime. He'd say, "It was so hot you could fry an egg on the sidewalk, and I'd run from the upper level of Grand Central Station, and I'd keep going, and I'd call on that customer and this customer."

Frank would fall on his face and lose $200,000 or $300,000, and then he'd contact Mother in Baltimore, and she'd send more money up to him. She was sitting there with her safe deposit box stuffed with stock certificates. She'd call the trustee and say, "Now, my son-in-law just needs about a quarter of a million dollars of this stock for a couple of months, he says, and he'll have it back by whatever." Then she'd send the money up to Frank, and it would go gurgling down into some bad investment and get swallowed, and then he'd go back to her again.

Things got pretty ugly at the end of our marriage. He'd say things like, "Arrgh! Who can get along with you?" and then he'd rip off his Rolex watch and hurl it into the fireplace. Or the old Raskolnikoff trick, throwing the Baccarat martini glass into the fireplace or against a wall. When I finally realized what Frank was doing with my money, it was too late. I went to a lawyer. There are a lot of attorneys out there who are looking for wealthy women who are devastated, and they'll come in and take what's left. They'll take advantage of the fact that you're shell-shocked. The attorney immediately hit me with, "I want a check from you for $30,000" (we're talking twenty years ago now) "and the whole fee within six weeks will be $60,000." I said, "How can you ask for that?" My husband had been fired from his job. What I had left in my hands was about $5,000. That was all I had.

Predictably, Frank continued his flim-flamming. He pursued a well-heeled divorcee who had a going real-estate business. He locked into the poor woman, made her some pitch that she obviously bought into for a while, and without risking marriage, he simply moved in with her. She put up with him for eight years, roughly half the time I'd lasted with him. Then after he had mismanaged her business, which he had wormed his way into, he was summarily dismissed by the woman and was once again snooping around, in his customary bloodhound fashion, for another victim. As I understand it from various trusted communications, Frank is currently targeting a wealthy widow for an eventual pounce. I haven't seen him in fifteen years, but I have ways of being kept informed of his dubious peregrinations.

What bothered me so much when my husband lost the money was the loss of my independence. I was going to be dependent on this woman — my mother — and she scared me to death from the beginning. Mother still had about $1.3 million, and that had to last both of us for twenty years. I had five children to put through four years of private school each, and then college. Someone reading this could say, "Well, why didn't you pull back?" I've had people say that to me. "Why didn't you send the kids off to work stuffing bags at a supermarket?" I was trying to beat the clock. My mother was then seventy-seven. She still had the house in Baltimore — a piece of property that was doing nothing but appreciating. I was trying to do for my children what had been done for me because I still think it's a benefit. I don't think it's a liability to have had what I had. It's what people sit around dreaming of. It's what makes people keep buying lottery tickets. I bought the lottery the day I was born.

Would I rather not have had that kind of money? Of course not! I was going to say I can be Spartan, but I don't think so. You know what I never liked? I'm not too good at roughing it — probably because of my background. Once I did something like camping. Uh uh. Oh no, please. Don't hand me something like a little tin thing out of a kit, and tell me, "There's a faucet behind that shed. Go over there and turn the thing," and rusty water comes out. Uh uh. No no no.

If there's a leitmotif, if there's a constant refrain that I've heard over and over, it is [mockingly]: "Well, how would *you* know? You've always had money." "Well, how would *you* know? You don't have to work for a living." Or: "Unlike you, *we* have to work for a living." "Oh, for God's sake, whaddya think? It grows on trees? It might for you, but it doesn't for us." I've always had a feeling of separateness, of being different. Different. Not part of just about everybody else. If I have a blind spot, which I would admit to, it is that I've never had any experience figuring out how to earn one dollar, let alone a million of 'em. I don't know how to dig a ditch for six hours and have somebody hand me $35. I don't know how to do something by the sweat of my brow. I shouldn't say I don't know how; I should say I've never done it.

But as I just said, I wanted my children to have what I had. Eventually, Mother's income wouldn't handle my expenses. You can go through a million in twenty years, and that's why she doesn't have anything left. A few years ago, I had to sell the small home I'd bought after I lost my estate to creditors. But because my funds were depleted so badly, I had to move down here to live with my mother and care for her until a year ago, when I placed her in a nursing home. Her inheritance is gone, of course. Her house is worth at least half a million, but I can't sell it until she's gone. If I didn't have a sense of humor, I'd either be dead by now or in some institution, wiping my nose on my sleeve. Mother is ninety-four, and she's hanging onto her life by a cobweb. Almost every week, the people at the nursing home think she's going to die. But her goal in life is not to die — ever. She plans to stay around interminably, indefinitely, eternally.

My story can be a fantastic lesson for anybody reading this book. And it can happen on a lesser scale. Money is the root of all evil in bad hands.

# Barbara Stanny

*Raised to be trusting and naive, Barbara Stanny believed that her job was to get married and produce children. Her husband would manage her wealth and take care of her. Not a moment too soon, Stanny discovered that her husband was gambling away her inheritance in a series of bad investments. Faced with monumental legal consequences, Stanny struggled to overcome her resistance to dealing with financial realities. Ultimately, she became financially proficient, and in fact, now trains other women to manage their assets.*

I found out I was wealthy when I was twenty-one. My parents flew me out to Las Vegas from Boston University, where I was a senior, in a private jet. We had a suite at Caesar's Palace, and we were sitting at breakfast eating lox and bagels and knishes. My father showed me a document, and it turned out to be my trust. He told me, "You are a very rich woman."

All I know is that it was a great feeling. A rush of warmth came over me, a heady excitement. But beyond that, it didn't mean anything to me; it just meant that I was safe. I was going to be taken care of. And if my father told me how much I was worth, I have no idea.

My father was very well known in the city where we lived — *very* well known. I'd be walking down the street, and I'd bump into somebody, and they would say, "Oh wow! You're so-and-so's daughter!" It was wonderful, and it was horrible. It was wonderful because I always felt important. Having so much money was great — we had a great big house with great cars. But at the same time, I always felt different. I felt lost. There was no me. I thought that people would either like me because of my father and the money, or they wouldn't like me. My own self disappeared into my father's big, big persona.

I remember signing financial documents in fifth grade, but I didn't know what I was signing. My parents never talked to me about money. They never explained things to me. I understand now that they were living in the days when you didn't explain money to little girls. My parents believed that little girls just didn't need to know. I didn't know how much I had until right before I got divorced. I am forty-five now, and I was maybe thirty-five then. It was a very arduous process of finding out.

Whenever I asked my parents about money, I got just one piece of advice: "Don't worry."

I was planning to go to graduate school and get an M.A. in art history, and I remember that on graduation day, my father took me out for lunch and said, "Well, what are you going to do?" I said, "I'm going to go to U.C. Berkeley and get my master's degree in art history." I was very passionate about it. And he basically said, "You know, that's a sweet idea, but it really isn't what you should be doing. You should be thinking about getting married and having children."

I'll be damned if I didn't meet my husband three months later. It was like I knew my father was right, so I got married. I knew David was looking for a rich woman, but he was so dazzling and handsome. I think he loved me, too. When we walked down the aisle, my parents breathed a sigh of relief, as if to say, "There is a man who will take of her!"

Well, that man did manage my money, but he did not take very good care of me. When my father had to communicate about an investment or some kind of deal, he would write to my husband. It was like I wasn't even part of it. I never balanced a checkbook, I never paid a bill, I never did anything connected with the financial part of my life. It was as if someone had amputated that part of me, you know? I just didn't understand. There was this mysterious, amorphous thing called "money and financial management." It was as if someone had put me in China, and everyone was speaking Chinese, and there were all these strange smells and strange customs. That was how I felt about money.

David turned out to be a compulsive gambler, and he was gambling with my inheritance! After we had been married seven years, I found out that he was making bets at the races. He'd lose a lot

86

of my money, and then he would swear that he'd never do it again. I would just say "okay" — and then it would happen again.

He continued to "take care of" our money, and I continued not to know what he was doing. It was a very addictive relationship. I was the co-addict, and I enabled him. It was very painful and frightening for me.

Towards the end of our marriage, I would go to the ATM machine, and there would be no money in my account. That wasn't supposed to happen! I mean, I was brought up not to worry. I didn't know where the money was, and I didn't know what to do. The terror I felt was paralyzing.

Around that time, my parents came out to California to visit me, and somehow they found out that David was at it again. My father said, "You know, if your husband cannot learn to manage your money, we are going to take it away from him." In that moment, I started to grow up. I said, "What about me? Why can't I manage it? And my father said, "Okay, go ahead," but both of us knew that I didn't know what to do. I said, "What do I do?" and he said, "Ask questions." And I said, "What questions do I ask?" and he said, "Whatever you want to know."

I got divorced, but I still had no sense of how much money I had. I started to learn about the specifics of my financial situation through a workshop at Resourceful Women in San Francisco. I also went to meetings, and someone suggested I talk to a financial planner. That idea had never occurred to me. So I interviewed seven financial planners, and I found one who was just wonderful. He told me what questions to ask, how much money I had, and what documents to get. But even after this wonderful man had explained my trust statements to me, I still couldn't understand them. I would look at those statements, and I just couldn't get it. It was a real sickness.

Then I got a letter from the State Franchise Tax Board. I couldn't understand it, so I put it aside. It happened to be in a stack of papers I brought to my accountant for my tax return, and he looked at it and said, "Sarah, this is serious. You'd better talk to your lawyer." It turned out that six years earlier, I had sold all my stock in my father's company — worth $3 million. I had let David take care of everything, and he decided not to declare the capital gains from that stock; he thought California taxes were too high. I don't know where he got off! So I got a tax bill for $583,000. Meanwhile, he had moved to England, where the taxman couldn't touch him. So I had to pay up. I found a lawyer who tried to get me out of it, but he couldn't do it.

After that, I had less money, and I was getting really scared. I said to myself, "I gave away my power, I gave away my responsibility, and now I've got to start understanding money." I talked to lots of people. I asked them, "How do I understand this thing called money?" They gave me names of books to read and they told me about classes I could go to. I did all the things they suggested, and damned if I still couldn't get it! I'd read a book, and my brain would clog up. I would just forget how much money I had.

Two years later, I got pages of gibberish in the mail, and I didn't even know it was another tax bill. I sent that letter to my father, who said, "Don't worry. It was addressed to your husband." Again, I just happened to save the letter, and my accountant saw it. Again, he said, "Barbara, this is serious. I think this is worse than the last one." So I went to a lawyer, and he told me that I owed the government almost $700,000 on account of some kind of tax shelter that David had bought which was declared illegal a year after he'd bought it. My biggest fear had always been that I was going to lose my money, and here I was, watching it go away. It scared the shit out of me. I mean, I had three children — I had to do something. That was when I knew that I *had* to learn. First of all, I found some better lawyers. And I called my father and asked him, "Will you help me if I have to pay this?" but he said no. To this day, he doesn't know why he wouldn't help me, but I think it was divine intervention. I think things have to get really bad before they will change. It was a crisis, and it was the best thing that had ever happened to me. I wish I had not gone through that pain and fear, but it forced me to take responsibility.

At the same time, I found a fabulous therapist. We worked really, really hard, and I got in touch with some deep, deep fears and beliefs about money. My therapist said, "I'm going to be one of your inner voices. Tell me how much you want to learn about money, and I'm going to talk back to you." So I said, "I really want to learn about money," and (speaking as one of my inner voices) he said, "No, you don't. You don't care about that stuff. You don't want to have anything to do with it." I tried to argue back, but then I realized,

"That's it! There *is* that voice in me." I learned that by dialoguing with the voice, it gradually stopped being so strident. Maybe it just wanted to be heard. Eventually, the veils lifted. I can't say that it happened quickly, but somehow the resistance wasn't so strong.

I decided that I would do a twenty-four hour meditation. I asked myself, "What do I need to get smart about money?" My goal was to have my answer at the end of the twenty-four hour period. I tried to clear my mind as best I could, to get to a place of total peace. And I didn't talk to a soul. When I came out of that meditation, I started writing in my journal: "I need a mentor. I need a teacher."

And so I found myself a mentor to teach me about money — a stock broker. He said, "We've got to invest a significant amount, but not enough that if you lost it, you would be hurt by the loss." We spent eight months working together, and we made every kind of stock-market investment possible. We put money in puts, we put money in calls, we shorted, we had convertible bonds, we had preferreds, we had closed-end funds, we had open-end funds. And I learned. He made me read through my transaction slips and activity statements. And when I didn't understand things, he would patiently explain them. It was great; it took away so much of my fear. It was only by doing that I learned. And now, investing has become such an integral part of my life: I eat, I sleep, I brush my teeth, I invest.

Somewhere along the line, managing my money became fun. It even became fascinating. I subscribe to twelve financial newsletters and five financial magazines. I go to seminars for financial planners because I love it. I get together with my friends, and we talk money. I even started an investment group for women, and I'm just beginning to go around giving talks. My current passion is to start doing financial education for women. Something magical has happened to me since I have gotten control of my money.

# David Bowman

*Raised with middle-income values, David Bowman was shocked when he inherited $2 million and found himself among the wealthy. His strong work ethic and sense of social responsibility were at odds with his privilege and his financial freedom. The question of work has presented special dilemmas for him: How can he ever live up to the high expectations which noblesse oblige confers on him? Must he work himself into the ground to "earn" his wealth? How can he learn to value his volunteer efforts? Recently, through the help of therapy, Bowman has given himself the chance to go to art school and pursue his talents.*

I grew up not knowing that my family was rich or that I too would be rich one day. We lived in a normal middle-class home, and we believed that we weren't that different from other people. My mother was a hard-working career volunteer for the YWCA and the church and lots of other committees. She also did everything for us, all the cleaning and cooking. We didn't have servants. We went to public school like everybody else, and my father was a public school teacher.

Both my parents' families have been in the United States for generations. My mother's family had property, but never great wealth. The wealth in my family comes from my father's side, going back over five generations. There was money from the paper industry on his mother's side, and from banking on his father's side. We lived in a small town because my parents didn't want to live in the nearby city where his family owned the mill, and everybody knew who my father was. I've heard my mother say she didn't like to go into stores in that city because if she said who she was, she would automatically be ushered over to the most expensive products.

My grandmother lived in what you could call a *nouveau* mansion, with acres and acres of lawn. She had maids and a groundskeeper. I was uncomfortable with that situation. It was kind of schizophrenic — feeling like we were more or less like everybody else, but having a grandmother who had servants working for her. Other kids with less money than me had bigger houses and more toys, and maybe went on more vacation trips. But their parents didn't pack up the whole family and go live in Africa for two years, like we did.

My father had a strong reaction against the wealth and everything that went with it. Both my parents had feelings about people who were ostentatious, who were into consumption. We grew up buying things on sale. We saved plastic bags and rubber bands, and we recycled cans and bottles. We didn't buy something new just because the other one was scuffed up, and we didn't get a new car every three years. We ran our cars into the ground. If anything, my father was even more thrift-oriented than my mother. I think it was a reaction to having had so much more than others when he was young.

It wasn't until I was in college, in the seventies, that I started to figure things out. There was this free-floating Marxist analysis of society going on at my college. I figured out that my father's extended family owned a whole paper company, and that a thousand people worked for us. One day, the family was called together to sign off on a settlement regarding ownership of shares and future control of the company. At that point, it became clear to me that not only did my grandparents own this company, but my generation was going to own it some day, and that we were already named in a series of trusts. It was one thing to have a grandmother who was owning class, who was rich; here I was at the age of twenty, only beginning to understand that I was from a wealthy family, and I was going to be wealthy just like they were. When I saw a poster that said "Eat the rich," I understood that my nuclear family would be part of the main course. And all of these things I'd heard about the aristocracy and the owners and the means of production — they were me! The rich people who exploit all the other classes and keep the profits for themselves, that was my family. We were among that one percent.

I understand that laws are constructed in such a way that rich people can retain their property and continue to pull economic strings so that they can get wealthier and wealthier, and that it's all legal. It's the way the system is set up. We supposedly live in a democracy, but in reality we live in a capitalist economic system. As far as I understand it, that means you can use your money and your position and your power and the law to make as much money off other people as you are able. You can take all the profit that you're allowed to take, and pay your workers as little as you can. And you can bend the environmental regulations or the work safety regulations. All of these things are bent by Congress to help business, and when you're helping business, you're basically helping whoever owns the businesses to keep their profit margins as wide as possible. All of these things are the fundamental values that our country lives on, swears by, bows down to, is organized under. I also understand that whole countries and whole continents and whole cultures are exploited for economic reasons.

The year I graduated from college, I inherited about $2 million in stock in the family company. I'm thirty-four, and I've lived on that wealth for eleven years. If I hadn't got the inherited wealth right out of college, if I had had to work for a living, I think things would have gone a whole lot better. It's exactly what my mother was afraid of, that the money would rob me of a certain kind of motivation to really show my stuff.

*For several years after college, David was involved with a number of projects — acting in political theater, singing in nursing homes, planning wealth conferences, and working with men's groups to put together slide shows and videos about the socialization of men.*

Sometimes I worked full-time for volunteer organizations, but more often, I worked part-time here and part-time there and had my finger in five different groups, projects, and committees. I'd be designing a flyer for one group, and helping out with a conference committee for another group, and doing publicity with a third group. I did all that work basically without being paid. I decided that I could use my privilege to "pay myself" to work for free. When I worked for a small theater company, I often forgot to cash my paychecks. I already had enough money, I was working very hard, and I was almost never free during banking hours. The ridiculousness of working for this tiny little wage and not even cashing the check was noticed, I'm sure.

I've had a real, real, real hard struggle with the idea of work and career and what I'm supposed to do with my privilege, with my time, with my responsibility as a privileged person. On the one hand, I was taught hard-working Protestant altruistic values along with a serious sense of guilt and responsibility, and on the other hand, I was given wealth and freedom. I felt like I had to save the world, I had to do good deeds. I felt like I had to give back what I had been given. My parents had taught me that we were just like everybody else, and we didn't have more money, and we weren't going to try to pretend to be better. But there was another message — that we *were* better. It eventually comes down to *noblesse oblige*. It was never talked about, but it feels to me like something that the wealthy class understands — that it's the responsibility of the wealthy to take care of other people, and we are sitting on the top of the pile, but we're there because we're the best, and we'll take care of all of you lesser beings.

That message was so subterranean in my upbringing: that we were the best people around, the smartest and the most moral and the most capable of judging what needed to be done. My parents probably aren't even aware of the ways that they are judgmental. That sense of superiority leads to a certain arrogance and a certain naiveté in myself — feeling like I'm the best person to lead, I'm the best person to sort it all out, I'm the most capable of making great things happen. So I'm expected to save the world, to be Jesus Christ and Gandhi and John F. Kennedy all wrapped into one. If you want to hear how absurd it is, they all ultimately failed, right? So I'm supposed to pull out the lessons of their lives and their self-discipline, and somehow do even more than they did — without getting killed. And the money allowed me to go on staring up that sheer cliff, thinking I could somehow jump from wherever I was to the top of it. I could go on believing I was capable of that, if I just decided which point to jump from. And when I talked to my friends and my family, I always had a line about what I was about to do, what I was working on, where my life was going, and all the big things I was doing. I was always doing enough work that I could talk about it. So I put out this bubble of motivation and productivity that was a big lie I had invented to protect myself from all these people knowing that I wasn't doing anything.

I feel like I've been really, really screwed up by the wealth, so that I couldn't even figure out how to work. I couldn't figure out how to get myself out the door into any of the numerous occupations I could have worked in. I could have done teaching, I could have done theater, I could have done graphics or layout, I could have done organizing. I'm good at things. I have plenty of skills and talents. But I've had this attitude that nothing I could do was quite good enough. Starting in an entry-level job wasn't good enough for me in terms of the great expectations I felt I had to live up to. So I've been sitting around trying to figure out how I would start some wonderful, amazing kind of social-change project, or some great theater company, or whatever. It would be okay for me to be a performer if I could somehow leap right into being a star, somebody that was known across the country for singing political music that inspires people. But I couldn't take the ten years I would need to actually accomplish that. And those ten years that I could have put into all kinds of occupations are now gone.

There was also a message from my parents about pleasure and self-control. Since we're the better people, we have to have self-control. So you can't pick an occupation that you would have too much fun in. You have to pick an occupation that is the most hard-working, most important thing to do. Even though my mother, of all people, was telling me to be an artist, I wouldn't allow myself to sit down and draw for ten minutes a week because that was fun. It was a "frivolous activity." I would have loved to be a performer. It's exactly what I wanted to do, but it wasn't acceptable behavior. Fun things are too selfish. Fun things are for after the work is done. For ten years, I didn't go to movies or play the trombone or dance. I would find myself watching television at two A.M. because it was the only time I didn't feel guilty doing it.

For ten years, I worked myself into the ground. My health got worse and worse and worse. After I had worked for the theater company about seventy hours a week for nine months, I crashed and never really got strong again. I was exhausted, but I was still trying to figure out how to be superman. I was just chasing my tail around and around and around, until finally exhaustion became a state of being.

In the last couple of years, I think I've made healthy decisions to continue to live on the wealth and let myself go to art school and get into therapy and allow myself to be who I am. Art school is filling my life with something, and somehow being a student is legitimate in its own right. I could look at it as prolonging not working, but eventually I will have to decide what I'm going to do after school. I'm trying to work something out in the next year. There's a question of whether I'm going to work full-time. Am I going to try to earn a living and pay all the things I need to pay? Or am I going to make it half-and-half? Or am I going to pay myself to do a certain kind of work?

Therapy has been great. Over and over for two years, the therapist has said to me, "The only thing you have to worry about is you. You have to love yourself first, or else you're not really much good for anybody else." And having the wealth makes therapy possible. The money is also making it possible for me to do anything that I'm led to do through the therapeutic process. I can set up exactly what my body and my soul need. It's a great relief.

# Francesca Da Silva

*The relationship between money and love is confusing for Francesca Da Silva. After growing up in a complicated family of "haves" on her mother's side and "have-nots" on her father's, Da Silva finds that sharing her wealth with her partner corrodes their love. Providing for her partner strips him of his self-respect, and their relationship becomes unbalanced. She believes that both partners must take care of their own financial responsibilities, yet how can she withhold her money without appearing to withhold love as well?*

Y ou can have a lot of money and feel so poor. And you can have a little money and feel rich. Without feeling grounded in my life — this particular small life that's mine — without feeling grounded in my house and the land and the animals around me, I wouldn't enjoy my wealth. Or maybe that is the real wealth — this place where I've luckily been able to land, like a little alien from outer space. I see people who are really wealthy, moneywise, often being horribly unhappy, and I don't associate myself with that state at all. I'm just not interested in that kind of unhappiness. Life is traumatic enough as it is.

All the money I've inherited came from my mother's side of the family. It went back to my mother's grandmother, my great-grandmother. The original pile was around $24 million. My great-grandmother's will was set up so that the men in the family get parcels of their money at thirty and thirty-five, and the rest of it at forty or forty-five. But the women are held under by this thing called the Victorian Clause. We don't ever get to touch our principal; we live off of the income. So I can't just willy-nilly ask for money and spend whatever I want. Although I've fought the terms of the trust for years, I have finally come to realize that I actually prefer it this way. I'm thirty-four, and I'm the only female in my generation. And I may be the only one that has any money left at this point!

My great-grandmother was a powerful woman. She was not a sedate little old lady. For her time, she was quite a rabble-rouser. She did things like put black children through school. We have a family tradition of powerful women, so the idea that she bought into the Victorian way of handling money was confusing to me. I cornered an uncle at one point when I was upset about the fact that all the men in the family had access to principal, and I didn't. He said, "It was set up that way because your great-grandmother thought that women were fools, and if they were to have access to their money, they would give it away — either to whomever they were in love with at the time or to some charity or religion. The money wouldn't stay in the family."

There is this thing about keeping the money in the family. My great-grandmother believed that the men were going to invest their inheritances and do business ventures. Even if they did nothing with the money, and it just sat there, they could at least pass it on to their children, who would retain the family name. But her fear was that the women would just let the money disappear from the family history. It would go out into somebody else's family. My relatives refer to family members as "agates" and nonfamily as "snot-agates" — a joke I have yet to figure out. It has something to do with a five-year-old saying, "Oh, it'/snot an agate." My family is bizarre that way. So "snot-agates" were not supposed to have access to the money.

There was some more money thrown in from my mother's father. He was poor when he married my grandmother, but he made a killing as a railroad-tie manufacturer during the heyday of railroad building. I think my grandfather always felt a little intimidated by my grandmother's wealth. She was unfailingly generous, which irritated him all the more. He was an obstinate self-made man, but he bought into all the regalia of having old money.

My father's family, on the other hand, is Italian working class. So I've inherited a funny combination of old-wealth attitudes and work-for-your-money attitudes, and both sets of attitudes have played a part in my life.

My parents lived as artists and bohemians. They moved to Paris when I was two, and we lived there for six years. My father taught painting. When his contract was up, he became fidgety, having grown up with class values which taught that if you're not working, your mind is going to turn into quiver. He wanted to go back to the United States to look for work, but my mother said, "Oh, Mummy will always support us. We can just stay here. You don't need to work." But he said, "No, you don't understand. I have to work." So he brought us back to Kansas City, and Mother stayed in Paris.

My grandparents did a lot of power-tripping with money. Whenever something displeased them, they would pull the money back from my mother. They did the same thing with my aunt. She was, and still is, beautiful — almost Amazon-like. She's almost six feet tall, and she's wild and really tough. When she moved to Greenwich Village, my grandparents cut her off: "We don't want you there. Come live near us." As a result, my aunt, after her wild period, never lived more than three blocks away from her parents. My mother and my aunt and my uncle all tried to find some way to escape the parental power-tripping around money. My uncle dealt with the whole issue by becoming a priest for twenty years. Between alcoholism and severe depression, my aunt has had to fight hard all her life.

Six months after my father and my brother and I moved back to Kansas City, my mother killed herself. She too suffered from depression and drug addiction, and I think ultimately her problems were tied to the money thing. When someone holds that kind of power over you, how do you break out from under it? From all accounts that I have ever heard, she was brilliant and witty. She was able to magnetize people into her circle and entertain them, but she couldn't turn that into something that was ultimately satisfying to her. I still don't know why she committed suicide.

The only reason my brother and I inherited anything at all is because my mother committed suicide. That is the most haunting aspect for me of having the money: What would have otherwise gone to her came to us. We got about $1 million each. I'm not extremely wealthy at all, although a million seems like a lot to me.

After my mother died, my brother and I went to live for two years with our rich grandparents. I was twelve. We would stay with our father on weekends. After those two years, we moved back in with him, thank God. My grandparents' house was in the poshest section of Kansas City. They had chauffeurs and three cooks and two maids.

The contrast between my grandparents' life and my father's life was extreme.

Although my grandmother had more money than my grandfather, he controlled her money. She received a weekly allowance of $500 from him. I couldn't believe that she kowtowed to her situation. One day, I found her allowance in the top drawer of his mahogany desk, and from then on, I would steal twenty dollars every week. I've always been a rebel. Then I'd go down to the store and buy games for the kids. I think my grandparents had to know I was doing it because I would come back every week with brand-new games, but no one ever asked me where I was getting the money. Isn't it strange? I think I actually wanted to get caught because that would have opened up the door on the abyss of money relations. And maybe that's precisely why nobody ever said anything to me.

There were things in my grandparents' house I still remember with fondness. My grandmother had a set of absolutely stunning hand-blown wine glasses painted with gold leaf. I've never seen glasses like that before or since. They were locked up in the basement. I used to steal those too. There was something about those heavily starched, crisp sheets I've always loved, and there was something about the beds. They were all really high and great fun to sleep in.

Grandmother had a room she called the Mary Poppins Room. She would buy presents for people all year long and stuff 'em in that room. Whenever cousin so-and-so had a wedding or a birthday, instead of having to run out and shop, she'd just go up to the Mary Poppins Room. Every once in a while, Rita, my grandmother's loyal Irish maid, would let my brother and me in there. There was a little pool table, and Rita would let us play around and investigate for a couple of hours, and then she'd shoo us out.

But I never felt like I would want to go back to that house or live that way. I never had a love for that house — other than the way a raven sees a shiny object in the distance and heads towards it. I think it's because the other part of my life was so much the opposite.

Visiting Grandma Rosa, my grandmother on my father's side, was a big contrast. She was a wonderful person. We used to go every Sunday to her house and play cards and read horoscope magazines. Every once in a while, she'd say things like, "Things are going to be tricky for you, but hang in there." Without ever having to say much, she communicated to me that she understood the money thing. I felt a tremendous amount of support and non-manipulative, non-power-oriented affection from her. When it was Christmas at her house, the focus was on enormous amounts of food, versus enormous heaps of presents at my other grandparents' house. We'd eat too much and have a great time joking with each other, and then pass out in front of the TV. Whereas Christmas with the rich grandparents was all about fancy wrapping and ribbons and a tree that you couldn't even see because it had so many ornaments on it.

My rich grandmother had three cooks, two of whom were black. Minerva had been a slave. She was just one of the most amazing people I've ever been around. I'd spend hours in the kitchen listening to her stories. Arlene, another black woman, made the best chocolate cookies I've ever had. Both the black cooks were big, motherly types, and Vesta was a skinny, proper Englishwoman. All three of them were amazing cooks.

There was a specific routine around dinner in that house. Every night there was a total feast, which it took all day to cook. Then the table was set with a white tablecloth, white linen napkins, silver, candles — the whole thing. All this fanfare around food was meant to cover up the fact that my grandfather never ate. He was so severely gone into alcoholism that his food just came back up again. He would kind of stir the food around on his plate and then excuse himself and throw up in the bathroom. He was one of these drunks you'd never know was drunk, as long as you didn't make him stand up or walk. It took me a long time to figure out what was going on. One day, he got up from the table, as he always did, and went to the bathroom. I followed him; he was throwing up. Then he would stay in the bathroom throughout the rest of dinner, and we would all sit at the table, pretending it wasn't happening. My grandmother would be leading the charade. It was important to her that his behavior was covered up.

Like everything else in my childhood, there were enormous contrasts in terms of the messages I got around money from my father and from my rich grandparents. My father was gentle and unassuming about the money because he knew inherently that you can't relay those messages in an obstinate fashion, or they don't get received. He used to say, "You don't have to take this all so seriously. You don't need to take on the whole guilt around the drama of your family and your mother's death and your aunt's insanity and who knows what your grandfather is all about. Just treat it as if you landed in this family, and you were handed this little pot of gold. You're just fortunate — that's all. It's like winning the lottery. Now you can do all the things you've always wanted to do."

The only communication about money I remember getting from my rich grandmother was: "You'll get a trust, and you'll get a piece of jewelry." And that was the end of the conversation.

The first time I gave money away to a boyfriend, I was fourteen. He had been in a car accident, and I gave him all the money I had saved from babysitting — $300. I was a good little working kid. He said he'd pay me back, but he never did. [Laughing uproariously:] It set the tone for the next twenty years! It's interesting that the dynamic of wanting to give money away — the guilt factor — affected me long before I actually got any money.

It wasn't until I met the man I would later marry that I realized I was going to enter into a long relationship with money vis-a-vis the person I loved. I didn't understand what that relationship would be, but it was obviously going to bear on my life. I was very romantic, and I wanted to support Daniel. "Oh, you're the great artist, and we can live together." Without knowing it, I did the same thing my mother had done. I have to give Daniel credit because he fought against me, also not really knowing why. He worked too, because he didn't like the idea of being kept. He'd say, "This isn't right. We shouldn't do it this way." We struggled with the issue of money for years and years. Then we travelled around Asia for a year and a half, and during that time, I was supporting him totally. I was so naive, I didn't have a clue. I did not understand why you can't just say, "Hey, I don't want this stuff any more than you do, so here — have some."

When Daniel and I came back from Asia, I bought this farmhouse. Being a city kid, I'd always wanted to get into working with the land. Our plan was that Daniel was going to work on his art — together we were going to build him a studio — and I was going to write. We both bought into the image that I had been creating, all along, of this wonderful little idyllic life. We'd do music together, and we'd do art together, and we'd be a creative, wonderful couple. Nothing in life would bother us ever again. We decided to get married. And the minute we got married, something strange happened. I started feeling like I didn't want to be alone in a house with one person day after day; I wanted to work and get out in the world. So I got a job waitressing, and Daniel didn't like that. Then things got bad between us, and we split up, but we didn't split up because of money issues.

The parallels with my parents' situation were amazing. My father, bless his heart, tried to warn me. He wrote me these long, painful letters, which I would read out loud to Daniel. I'd say, "Goddamn my father! What's he trying to do? Why is he imposing on my life?" Years later, I found those letters, and I understood that he was trying to help me. Eventually, his message got through, but it has taken me a long time, because I proceeded to repeat the situation two more times.

Next I got hooked up with Lucas, who ran an arts center. He was a charismatic leader with the ability to get people to believe in what he was saying and work hard for him. I supported his vocation and immersed myself in his ambition. For the first two years Lucas and I were together, I wrote grant proposals for him. I learned a lot: I learned how to run computers, I learned how to keep books, I learned how to fund-raise. I also gave a huge amount of money to the arts center — $80,000 over the course of three years. And for me, that's a lot. My best friend tried to warn me, but I'm thick and stubborn. Finally I woke up and realized what I was doing, so I extricated myself from the situation.

Then I went from the whole ordeal with Lucas straight into Michael. Right off the bat, I did the same thing again. Like both Daniel and Lucas, Michael was self-supporting, but marginally. And I immediately said, "Come live in my house." It was easy for us to live together, but at the same time, I let the veils of comfort fall too quickly. After we started living together, Michael stubbornly refused to go out and work. He just wanted to concentrate on his art and have me support him. I even bought him a big red truck for $20,000 so that he could cart his sculptures around. And then I panicked and said, "Hey, you promised to help me pay for this truck, and now I'm paying it off all by myself and resenting it." But he just dug his heels in further. He'd say, "Yeah, yeah, I'll look for a job," and then weeks would pass, and nothing would happen. It took me four years to pay off that truck — $500 a month. It was very painful every time I had to write the checks because it meant that I wasn't going to get any clothes or any dental work done that month. My trust pays about $35,000 a year, and that's wonderful for one person, but when you start divvying it up between two, it's tight. So every time I wrote those checks and every time I looked at the truck, I was forced to assess what I was doing.

About a year ago, I started questioning things intensely. All that questioning led to me to a decision that it was time for me to stop doing this. There was no reason for me to be so ashamed of having this small amount of money that I had to turn an otherwise brilliant human being into a mild lapdog. So I made the decision that Michael and I should part ways in terms of our living situation. I didn't want to end our relationship, and we've gotten along a lot better since I made that decision. Suddenly his creative juices are flowing again, and we're both enjoying each other. A large amount of honesty got punched into the situation. He has the truck. I don't want to look at it again.

I think, unfortunately, that I will have to do the narrow path for a while — live alone. I think my pattern around this issue is so ingrained and such a fix that it would be easy for me to slip right back into it. I need to explore the idea of being my own artist and my own lover and my own housekeeper. Not with the expectation that it's ever going to get perfect, because it isn't. I just want to see what happens if I allow myself the space I've never given myself. Since I was fifteen, I've always been with someone.

It's harder for me to respect a man when I'm supporting him. If I ever get involved with a man again, which I assume will happen, he's going to have his own money, or his own means of supporting himself. I don't want to have anything to do with that aspect of it again. It's not that I want anyone to give me more than what I have; I've got plenty. But I don't need to do that for someone else. It eats away at the love, and that's the part that hurts the most. It's not the money, it's the eating away of the love. It's insidious. I had a fantasy that a long way back this money was made off of a slave farm. The insidious quality of the money is so apparent in my family drama. It's amazing how that insidious quality has continued to linger!

There's also a male-female dynamic going on. If the roles were reversed, that dynamic would perhaps be more traditional, and therefore a little bit easier. I find that men in general are greedy to share my money, but at the same time, they aren't able to handle it well. It affects their self-esteem and their ability to maintain their ambition. I think it's somewhat peculiar to men because of the emphasis that's put on them to be ambitious. I think that for women, it's still a little bit fuzzier, so adding another fuzzy factor is no better or worse than it already was. But for men it creates havoc with their sense of self.

I've always had a middle-class compulsion to work for my money. I didn't inherit anything until I was twenty-two. Before I got my inheritance, I liked money, and so I worked for it, and I saved it. But I'm not good at the nine-to-five, everyday thing. The whole reason civilization was set up is so that we wouldn't have to work so hard, so that we could be artists, so that we could garden more. Sometimes I work out there in the world, and other times I work at home. When I'm working at home, I keep to a schedule. I'm actually very disciplined, and I get a lot done. I work on my writing, I work in my garden, and I study herbal medicine. Except for the writing, which has always been there — my secret love affair with myself — these other things, like studying herbal medicine, are fairly new. I don't feel like I'm dabbling because I'm genuinely interested, but it has taken me a long time to get there. I'm just learning to crawl.

It's also important for me to work outside of home. If you're an artist, the work world and the work ethic provide stability, and if you don't plug into that, ego reigns supreme. You become so self-involved that you can't see your own goals any more. Being in the world helps me sharpen my own ideas. I also love being with people.

I also want people to *see* that I'm working. When someone asks me, "What do you do?" if I don't have a job, I cringe and feel embarrassed and usually make something up. Michael's interesting that way because when somebody asks him what he does, he just says: "I'm working really hard on some projects at home." He has a lot of self-confidence about what he's doing, whereas even though I work hard at home — probably harder than a lot of people work at their jobs — I don't have the self-confidence to say, "This is as valid as your nine-to-five shit job."

Making the money become more mine has been another important challenge for me. I'm no longer as willing to give it away to somebody else because I think other people deserve it as much as I do. Having always felt guilty about being rich, I've longed to get rid of it. If I could just spread it around, it wouldn't be so haunting. But I discovered that the more I tried to throw it away, the more it haunted me. Obviously, everybody deserves to have a pot of gold, but there aren't that many pots. And I think that feeling more ownership of the money will help me to be wiser, and I'll be able to give more thoughtfully. Generosity of spirit is the heart of wealth.

So what does wealth mean to me? There's my land, and then there's being happy with the wealth. And then there is giving, which I have gone to both extremes on — supporting individuals and supporting organizations. I want to find my place somewhere in the middle. I'm looking for something that my heart is genuinely attracted to. Then I wouldn't be giving the money away out of guilt, or good riddance. The spirit of giving should be equal to the amount of money that's being given, instead of the money being much greater than the spirit, or vice versa. Finding that balance will mean that I have finally understood wealth.

# Kate Shepherd

*Kate Shepherd's biggest challenge as an inheritor has been to fill the emotional and spiritual void she felt growing up. She equates having wealth with the deadening effects of overprotection and pressure to maintain the status quo. She sought a much-needed adventure by trying to bicycle across the country, but it wasn't until she took on the rigorous commitments of marriage and motherhood that she began to feel fully alive.*

I have finally started to see wealth as a root cause of much of my life, as opposed to just another factor. It feels like most of who I am — my sense of being outside of life, my perfectionism, my focus on image, my feeling of being special, my difficulty with motivation or staying with something when it's hard, the trouble I've had waking up my heart and caring deeply about people, or about myself, for that matter — most of that started from the experience of growing up with a lot of money. It's like living in a bubble.

I was born into a big midwestern clan. My great-grandfather made millions in minerals. Both my great-grandfather and my grandfather had strong, charismatic personalities. They were men of big passions — tyrannical, driven, and gruff. My grandfather died before I was born, but he was an enormous presence and influence in the family. He'd tell his children that he would give them a quarter if they could run around the house in the snow in their bare feet. He had old-fashioned ideas about how to instill character. Character was a big thing, as was responsibility. He detested "weakness" of any sort. He was not at all sympathetic to artistic temperaments, which three of his four of his children have, including my father. To my grandfather, business was all.

My mother did not come from wealth; she is from a small farming town. So when she married my father, she ran smack into the family's wealth and power — and my grandmother. Mom really got the message from her mother-in-law that any woman who married into the Shepherd family had to be a certain way. She was expected to be socially involved in the community, she had to be a good volunteer and support charitable causes in the arts, and she had to be elegant. Grandmother basically communicated to her: do what I tell you to do, and live the way I think you should live. Grandmother would take Mom shopping and tell the saleswomen what looked good on her. It was extremely painful for Mom. Grandmother even picked out furniture for Mom and had it delivered to the house.

But Grandmother was magnificent to her grandchildren. I adored her. My most special memory is of Saturday night visits with her. My grandmother was artistic, and her house was extraordinary. There was a circular stairway that had a tree growing up through its center. That house was so exotic! She had boxes full of costumes and old artifacts, and my sister Annie and I were allowed to rummage around and dress up in costumes and play pretend. The three of us would have our dinner on trays, sitting in these big straw wingback chairs, and we'd pretend that we were on a ship. Annie and I were supposed to decide what country we were going to sail to. The whole thing was like something out of a storybook.

Sometimes we'd have flaming Baked Alaska for dessert, and then my grandmother would turn on the music, and the three of us would dance. Then Annie and I went to bed under these huge, huge quilts, and Grandmother would read us stories. The next morning, we would get up at six o'clock and climb in bed with our grandmother. I don't know how she did it, but by the time we arrived early in the morning, she would be up and looking elegant. She would have on a green silk bedjacket, and her sheets were of silk and satin. It was out of a movie.

My grandmother had a big influence on me. She was everything I could have asked for in a grandmother, and she reinforced the idea that I was special. From her, I got a feel for what kind of life I was supposed to live.

At a family meeting a few years ago, my father and his three siblings broke the pattern of just "doing business" and instead talked about their parents, both of whom had died by then. It was a moving, painful, and beautiful thing to hear and see how deeply these people had been shaped by their parents. I swear my grandparents seemed so fully present in the room that we decided not to have our next family meeting at the lake where we all have our summer places. The ghosts were just too real.

My mom's side of the family was just plain down home — as Scandinavian and Lutheran as you can imagine. They were simple, good people. I loved our visits to the little farming town where my mother's parents lived. I thought we were the hot-shit, special visitors from the city. Those visits were so relaxed. I think I had more genuine fun — just gathering ground cherries with my grandmother, playing in the cornfields, making up games with the Lutz kids, going to the creek — doing normal things — than I had in most of my growing-up time, which was full of structured fun. Everything was planned — ski trips, tennis camp, vacations in Europe. Fun was rarely spontaneous. When I was with my grandparents and our small-town friends, I sensed something more genuine and human — more real. I really just wanted to be seen for who I was, and that so rarely happened. In that little town, all pretenses evaporated. No one was really all that interested in who the Shepherd family was. So in spite of my illusion that I was hot shit, I really wasn't perceived that way by the Lutz kids or my grandparents or by the people who worked at the local dime store. For me, that came as a relief. Apparently, people liked me just for being me . . . because I was fun? Because I could giggle just as hard as other kids? Because I could act dumb and silly? Who knows? And my feeling was, who cares?

I never felt as comfortable with the Shepherd side of the family, and I always felt a kind of tension in myself. I used to wonder: Am I more a Shepherd? Or am I more a Lindstrom (my mom's maiden name)? Temperamentally and physically, I am more like my mother. But I have also latched on to being a Shepherd because of all the perks that go with it. So I have felt this internal conflict a lot in my life — who am I, really? Am I more a down-home person, or am I an elegant, refined rich person? More recently, I've been moving away from trying to figure out if I'm one or the other. I'm seeing both families in myself, and fortunately, it's starting to feel more enriching than confusing.

The house I grew up in was big and elegant and formal. Because it wasn't as huge as some houses I'd seen, I thought it was ordinary. It was not a house where you could just come in and kick off your shoes and feel comfortable. I remember not wanting to invite my friends over, and I couldn't even leave my things lying around in my room. I've internalized that to the point where I'm overly perfectionistic. That's why I love spending time at my sister-in-law's house. I mean, the TV's always on, and there are vague messes all over. They're not slobs, but their house is real and lived-in, with real people moving around — yelling every once in a while, hugging every once in a while.

I had a sheltered life. My mom was a devoted mother, and my sister and I received a lot of love and affection. I went to the "right" nursery school, and then to a private girls' day school from first grade right up through graduation. And there were great benefits for me. I have old, dear friends I feel very connected with, and I have a strong sense of rootedness in my home town. For a long time, I believed that I had an idyllic childhood. But when I look back, I see how narrow my childhood was. I didn't get the kind of exposure that would have made me ready for life outside of that limited world of affluence.

When I was around sixteen, my sister and I went downtown to the family office, and my uncle Harvey brought out some balance sheets. He told my sister and me what we were worth. He showed us some numbers, and he explained the basic concepts of our trusts. He told us that the trusts were for our benefit, to make sure that somebody wouldn't try to marry us for our money. What kind of a mind produces that suspicion? What kind of a mind thinks about using people in those ways? — not that it's a completely unfounded fear. I later found out that my aunt and one of my cousins had been married for their money. Now I'm getting over my fears for the most part, but there were times before I married my husband when I wondered, "What's his motivation?" There was also another message that came from the trust arrangement which I only realized much later: if someone might want to marry me, it must be for my money, because I'm not really lovable, just in and of myself. And that doubt is devastating.

That visit to the family office was the first time I had heard any figures. Before that, I never knew how rich we were. When I got home, I told my parents, "I hate this! I hate having all this money! I can't stand it!" My mother silenced me. Having grown up without wealth, she just could not understand why somebody wouldn't be completely grateful for their money. I was upset because I felt that my money separated me from everybody else. It made me feel different. There's this weird double bind that I think wealthy people get caught in. On the one hand, you want to be special. You've been taught that you're special, and you get into it. Who doesn't want to be special? On the other hand, you believe that you're different, and it feels wretched. I was really feeling the wretched part of the bind at that point. But boy, I was told not to complain about being wealthy — ever!

So in addition to not complaining, I tried not to think about being rich. It felt like I had to suppress a lot of direct questions, expressions of embarrassment, and anxiety in order to fit into my social role as a wealthy person. But after a number of years, I just couldn't do that mindless routine anymore. I became really involved in consciousness-raising in all areas of my life, including my wealth. So I started asking myself what it really means to have inherited money. I've had to work hard in the last decade to take seriously my own discomfort with being an inheritor.

I also remember feeling relieved that day at the family office when I was sixteen. I was glad that someone was there to protect me. It took me so long to get to the point where I could even figure out that the belief that I needed to be protected from gold diggers could be a problem. One of the family rules is that we should all be grateful to the family office, which does such a good job taking care of us. It's a bow-down kind of attitude.

That gratitude is crucial in the family. A few years ago, at one of our annual family meetings, my cousin Hillary was brought up as an example of an irresponsible spendthrift. My uncle said, "If we didn't have these irrevocable trusts, then what happened to Hillary could happen to any of us." Hillary had basically spent all her money on drugs, sex, and rock 'n roll, but because some of her inheritance had been held in trust for her, she will never be totally penniless. Then I piped up and said, "Yeah, but what about having control over your destiny?" It seemed to me like a deep split showed up in the family at that point, and I could sense almost energetically which people shared my feelings — not many. And Hillary's brother and father said, "Oh no, we are so grateful! It's a good thing that she is being taken care of."

The whole financial structure of the Shepherd family is built on enabling. This system is presented under the auspices of being a compassionate and valuable protection, but what it really means is that nobody has to take control of their lives — financially or in any other way. When you're rich, nothing matters because you can always pay away your mistakes. You don't even have to get into that risky territory where you might make a mistake. The whole system is infantilizing. Although we were brought up that way, at a certain point each of us has to choose whether or not we want to stay infantilized by the money.

There were a lot of unspoken messages or rules about wealth in my family. I think I must have learned them mainly by observing. One message was: Don't dip into principal. Another one was: Don't overspend lavishly. Don't piss away your money, and (what would be even worse) don't become degenerate. Don't talk about your money was another rule. Another one, connected with the "don't talk" rule, was: Be careful not to get taken for your money. And specifically, don't let a man marry you for your money.

It's fine to give money for charity, but we're not supposed to go too far out. The traditional, old-money causes are encouraged. So the symphony is fine, and education is fine. There is a family foundation that gives to traditional causes here in Cleveland. But to give money for social change or to support the rights of Natives or the gay-lesbian movement — those things don't fly very well.

The rules have more power because they are so unspoken. Because they have been taught to us as the things we shouldn't do, these rules keep getting broken. Family members seem to want to do what they're not supposed to do, like kids who want to explore exactly what they're not allowed to explore. A few people in the extended family have been married for their money, and a lot of people in the family have let themselves get taken for their money.

I was supposed to grow up to be proper, good, polite, well-groomed, well-educated, and totally noncontroversial. I was trained to become a perfect little society person. The pathetic thing is that I actually did that for awhile. I was a good girl and a good student, and I went to a good, elite women's college in New England. At college, it wasn't all that hard to keep my world-view reinforced. There are a lot of rich girls at that college — a lot of rich girls! Any time I was feeling different in comparison to my two best friends, who were not at all wealthy, I could remind myself of ten other girls I knew who had gone to the same kinds of private schools I had gone to. Some even had chauffeurs pick them up at the airport. I could always think of somebody who was a thousand times richer than I was, or who had a stuffier lifestyle than I had. Whether it was accurate or not, I saw myself as somewhere in the middle in terms of wealth.

After graduating, I moved to Philadelphia. I shared an apartment with a college friend, who did not come from wealth at all. She was busting butt working two jobs. I, on the other hand, bought my underwear at Bonwit Teller. I had a season's ticket to the symphony, I had my own car, and I had a job at a teacher-placement service for private schools. I was still in that narrow world I had grown up in. My roommate didn't have a car; she always went to work on the bus. If I was going to be late for work, I would just drive my car to the city and pay fifteen dollars to park it downtown for the day. Or I'd park it in a twenty-minute parking zone. I probably racked up twenty-five parking tickets that year. My car was booted and towed two or three times. I just thought it was a joke. Once I naively left $300 in cash from my first paycheck on a bench in the locker room at the YWCA where I went swimming, and when I came back, the money was gone. I was sorry, of course, but the loss didn't make even a dent. That money was purely symbolic for me. I was totally out of touch — not only with the world, but also with the emotional and financial necessities of my peers.

My mom got me set up with the Junior League. I went to a few meetings and parties, and I did a few little internships here and there. Once I worked with abused children in a lousy part of town. I didn't really have a function — I'd just talk to a few kids, and that was it. I was trying to make that kind of thing work for me, but I just couldn't. I finally decided, "This is not for me." It's not that I had tons and tons of things that *were* me — that was where I felt the pain.

So I went to the next rung up on my mental ladder of things I thought I was supposed to do. I remember my uncle — the one who runs the family office — saying that he didn't care what we did, as long as we were contributing something positive to society. So I decided to be a teacher, which felt a little more useful than the Junior

League. My parents had been teachers, so it was a family-approved profession. I could afford to teach at a little private school where they paid me $9,000 a year. I was thrilled. I spent far more than I was making just on my rent.

I never really put myself into that job. The teacher in the next classroom was forever spicing up her curriculum, and she found her job interesting and challenging because she invested her heart in it. But I used the same assignments again and again. I was doing as little work as possible, so of course the job wasn't satisfying.

I started doing a lot of addictive things. I ran like a maniac and actually damaged my legs. I think I ran a lot so that I could justify eating a lot — I was never satisfied, and I was trying to fill up some huge void inside. I wanted to do something big and bold; I wanted to prove myself in a way that didn't have anything to do with my money. I wanted to feel alive — things were so muted out. I felt like nothing spontaneous had ever happened to me, that I had never had any adventures. Even our family's trips to Europe, which would have been a big adventure for a lot of people, were so staid. Everything was first class; there was no challenge, there was never any possible threat to our comfort and safety. The most exciting thing that happened was getting food poisoning in Austria and throwing up for a day.

A friend of mine went off to the African jungle with the Peace Corps, and I wanted my adventure too. I was thinking about riding my bike across the U.S., so I talked to a woman who had done that. She said, "You know, you can eat whatever you want while you are biking because you'll burn off so many calories." So I decided: "This is it. This is what I'm meant to do."

I flew to Seattle. I spent quite a bit of money to get the equipment I needed — a tent, maps, and so on. It's not that it didn't occur to me that cross-continental biking might be dangerous, but in a bizarre way, the danger was what I wanted to embrace. Of course, my family mobilized to try to make me change my mind. But their efforts to convince me to stay safe only backfired. I wanted to rebel even more. Thank God there was at least a smidgen of rebellious energy that hadn't died in me.

The day I started out on that bike trip, I ate a huge waffle breakfast. Then I pedaled for about four days. I camped out at night, and I got extremely lonely. One day I was sitting at a picnic table in Who-knows-where, Washington. A motorcycle gang was hanging out at the next table, and I almost approached them — I was so lonely. I remember writing about that moment in my journal: I thought it was really sad that I was considering hanging out with those people — just for some company. That was a painful moment of truth for me. I didn't want to acknowledge to myself that I wasn't the adventuresome type, and that this whole fantasy was coming from a very sad place inside of me — an empty place.

My trip ended prematurely at Ellensburg, Washington, where a branch of my family has land holdings. My uncle had arranged for me to stay in the family's lovely, posh condominium, and I was treated royally by the property managers. Here I was, trying to have a non-wealth-related adventure, but to tell the truth, I was so relieved that I could step back into privilege. I also felt defeated. I wished that I didn't have such a longing for the kind of comfort and privilege I was greeted with. Because I *had* been stretched in some ways by those four days of biking, and I did have some adventures.

I went home at that point. My bike wasn't working right, my knee wasn't working right, my father needed to have surgery, and my mother wanted me to come back. Those were perfect excuses, which I was looking for to save face. I could go home and not have to admit the real defeat — an inner, spiritual defeat.

I felt like that trip literalized my inability to make anything positive or authentic happen in my life. I experienced, physically and geographically, my directionlessness, my lostness. I didn't have much sense of self, and I didn't have any practical experience of living without comfort. I didn't even *want* to live without comfort. You know how people who have a lot of struggles to deal with in life, especially money struggles, often end up developing solid, strong character? I had not developed any of that. I thought, "Hey, if I can't deal with the physical challenges, who am I? What have I got?" Here was my one chance to stay alive, and I was succumbing to dying — again.

That had been such a recurrent experience in my life: the pressure was so powerful to maintain the status quo, to be safe, to be good, to do what had been done before. The lure of luxury, of comfort, of security was so powerful that I wasn't able to let the other parts of me come out.

I did manage one other adventure: I went to Findhorn in Scotland. Those people were living totally alternative, radical lifestyles. They weren't cocooning in their suburban ranch houses or going to the country club — they were living communally and simply. They had huge gardens, they talked to the *devas* in the gardens, and they grew enormous asparagus and tomatoes. I was titillated by the spiritual stuff, but what moved and inspired me most was that those people were able and willing to make sacrifices. They didn't have to have a lot of money. They looked healthy and fulfilled, and their hippie children were happy. I'm sure I'm idealizing it, but compared with the lifestyle I'd grown up with, Findhorn represented a totally different way.

I stayed at Findhorn for a week. I worked in the gardens, and I felt challenged because I couldn't just throw my dirty clothes in the washing machine at my convenience. I actually broke the rule for using the washing machine; I was leaving the next day, and I wanted to have clean clothes. Someone confronted me about it. I realized then that the spoiled part of me had been thinking, "I'm different. I don't have to obey these rules like everybody else. You guys do, but I don't." My sense of privilege was rearing its ugly head. That voice of privilege has always been there, and I have to make a conscious effort to silence it. I have to tell myself, "You know what, Kate? That rule applies to you too." I've been humbled a number of times by people who have confronted me about that kind of thing.

I have five trusts, and the assets from those trusts add up to about $5 million. Some of the trusts are revocable, and some are irrevocable. Everybody's irrevocable trusts are managed by the office; they're invested collectively. They're all in an incredibly complex interrelation to one another, so that we can avoid a lot of taxes, and so that we can get "bulk rates" on investments.

It would be conceivable for me to go through my entire life and never balance my checkbook. I wouldn't have to spend any time at all managing my money. And any time I bounce a check because I haven't balanced my checkbook, any time I find myself close to running out of money before the end of the month, it's so easy to call the family office and say: "Could you send $2,000 more before next month?" Marge, the secretary, can wire it to me in a day. I could even have set it up with the office to have them pay my bills, but I haven't done that.

So much is done for me. My monthly checks go right into my bank account. We're supposed to pay our own credit card bills, and when we buy a house, the office recommends that we get a mortgage so that we are aware of the value of the house. I think that's a superficial, compensatory measure to cover over the fact that our family never took full responsibility for educating us about what our money means or how to handle it. I still don't really understand the value of my house, and I've never earned much of my mortgage. I think a lot of my frustration and anger come from realizing how little I was trained to deal with my wealth. Nobody prepared me. I feel ashamed about how little I know — even now.

That's a big issue for me these days. Whenever I've asked questions about my investments, my uncle Harvey and my cousin Chester can't seem to answer them in layman's terms. I can lose the meaning of a whole sentence because I don't know one word. My uncle is baffled that so few of us call and ask questions, and I have suggested to him that if you're forty, and all your life somebody has always managed your money for you, why start now — when it's so much easier to just stay uncurious and get that check every month?

I finally decided I needed somebody outside the family who would explain these things to me in simple terms. So now I have a team of investment counselors who manage my revocable trust for me. When I was trying to decide if I wanted to refinance my house when the interest rates were so low (I wouldn't even have known to pay attention to interest rates, except that my husband suggested it would be a good thing), I called my financial advisor and asked him: "Which is better, this rate or that rate?" And he straightforwardly told me it was six of one, half a dozen of the other. It was exactly the kind of clear, direct answer I'd been waiting to hear all these years.

It has been good to get advice from somebody who's not in the family. There's a myth in our family that relationships, family dynamics, are completely separable from money. I'm astounded at how long we've bought into that illusion. People think we can have a business meeting that has nothing to do with who we are, how we relate to each other, and how we feel about ourselves. I keep trying to shatter that myth at every meeting I go to; I keep saying it's bullshit.

Finally, my cousin Chester, who manages the office, is catching on. He's a member of my generation. When I describe my dilemmas around wealth, they're not foreign to him. He's the only one in the family who has taken charge of the money; he works with it daily. So he's not afraid of it, he feels fully empowered. He has also proved to himself that he can make a good living using his own talents.

I have a fantasy that the only way I'll learn about this money stuff, the only way I'll become a better person, is to lose all my money. Then I'd be punished for having it in the first place. Guilt and a need to be punished are such pervasive ingredients in our family dynamic. Except for Harvey and Chester, none of us earned this money ourselves, and even they didn't earn as much money as they have. I think the rest of us know, deep down, that there is something unjust about having all this money. So the trick for me is to get beyond that guilt to a point where I can feel empowered, so that I can really use the money. I want to be able to see and use the money as a resource.

There are only two things I feel I really "own" in my life. One is my marriage, because the love and the commitment come out of me. My marriage wasn't just given to me. And the other one is my spiritual work — it's completely mine (although the money that's paying for it isn't mine).

I guess some people who have found spiritual paths that feel right to them know the experience of "I'm home." That's the feeling I've had ever since I connected with the small group I'm involved with. It's an approach that combines psychological work with spiritual practice. It feels right for me — largely because of the honesty. Much of my experience as I was growing up felt dishonest or inauthentic, and that's my biggest gripe about growing up with money. It fosters inauthenticity. It has separated me from the grist of life. I just wanted something that was real. And now I feel as though a gradual, subtle, sort of organic shift is going on inside me — from inauthenticity to authenticity.

I also appreciate this spiritual work because I can't just retreat from it. My wealth is no protection for me. In meditation, the money doesn't help me not fall asleep or not feel my profound anxiety or not see my mind running like a rat in its cage. The money allows me to pay for weekend programs so that I can do longer periods of meditation, but it sure doesn't help me in emotional process groups, when the heat is on and I have to feel something I don't want to feel. Having money doesn't help me one iota with that. In fact, some of my most powerful breakthroughs have come when I was being confronted by other group members about the superiority I feel because I have money.

The decision to get married was hard to make. It's not that I haven't had relationships before, but I've never been willing to take a risk. I never put myself in situations where I could have failed. I succeeded in everything I did. I never took up anything I wasn't good at. I got a lot of strokes for being a good girl, for being a good student. Allowing myself to bring my heart along and really risk something where I might be a failure or look silly or fall flat on my face is something I've never tried until recently.

I haven't given Rocky any money yet, but we both know that when his money runs out, I will be the one supporting the two of us. I don't want to enable him because it's so destructive to his sense of self-respect, to my respect for him, and to my respect for myself. Enabling with money is incredibly crippling. So I find myself at sea as to how to handle these things so that we both have our integrity. Both Rocky and I have to deal with our prejudices about a woman supporting a man. It's entirely different when a man is supporting a woman. Mom and Dad had their issues, but their entire social set gave the nod to their relationship.

Rocky wants me to show that I trust him completely by sharing half of everything I have. In his mind, that is part of what a marriage is. And in the same breath, he says, "I know that if you were to do that, it would fuck up our marriage." If I were to give him half of what I have, he would resent it deeply, and he would feel disempowered. When I pick up the tab for certain things, like trips and entertainment, his self-esteem plummets, he gets lazy, and he doesn't assert himself. The whole thing spirals down until we are at each other's throats. We have gotten to the point where we understand that that is the emotional reality between us right now.

I'm learning to let Rocky know I trust him emotionally. He is willing to talk things through, he tries to get over his defensiveness as fast as he can, and he tells me the truth. But for me to trust him financially would mean that he would need to trust himself financially first. And he admits that he doesn't trust himself when it comes to money. So it is a delicate situation. It's not as simple as looking at some self-help book and saying, "Let's find a money strategy we want to try." We need to look at what happens from day to day, and we need to look at the quality of our relationship. There is a different atmosphere in the house when Rocky is earning money and using it to pay his expenses. For example, we have gone on a couple of trips that I paid for exclusively. He put nothing into those trips — emotionally or logistically. He went into his passive, complaining mode. But when he is investing some of his money, he is a lot more likely to invest something emotionally. I'll say, "How about if I pay three quarters and you pay a quarter, and you do the planning?" We are in a constant state of experimentation.

It's just a big old messy journey that we've decided to go on together. I haven't wanted anything to be messy in my life — nothing! — and here I married into this incredibly messy situation with a man who has children from two other women. But I finally feel like I am coming into life and lowering some of my demands that life be something other than what it is. And [crying as she speaks] I feel consistently grateful for that. It is very moving to me.

I have a child now, and for the first time in my life, I feel a sense of connectedness and community with other people — a connectedness that has nothing to do with money. Everyone who gets up in the middle of the night with a child has a common bond. I guess you could pay your way out of it by hiring a nanny, but that is not a choice I have made — or would ever make. I wouldn't want to be excluded from that particular kind of involvement. I *want* to change diapers, I *want* to deal with my kid's tantrums, I *want* to do the nitty-gritty.

This is the single most important thing I want to say about how my wealth has affected me. Until I got married and connected with a spiritual path, I always felt like a spectator of life, like I was somehow on the periphery, watching life happen to other people, watching them include their souls in some way. The truth is that unless I give all my money away, I will never be in a position where my safety and my comfort are at stake. What I want to say to other heirs is, "Accept the fact that your safety or your comfort will probably never be at risk.

Accept that you will always be comfortable and secure materially, and then shift the sphere. Go to a sphere where you have do something at stake, and your money can't help you. It might be a relationship, where your heart is on the line. Or it might be something like going off and meditating in a hut somewhere, where there is nothing you can do to buy your way out of the anxiety you feel about not being able to find God. Whatever it is — shift the context.

"The money is just a fact of your life. You will always be able to find the exit door in the physical realm. You can climb mountains and that kind of stuff, you can set yourself up to do that, but in some sense, those adventures are contrived. You will never really have to face the possibility that the next economic downturn could put you out of your job, and you and your family could be on the street. But you can find a realm to move into where you can feel exposed."

What I needed was to know that I was entering into some experience that would draw exclusively on my own inner resources. That is what my marriage does. My money doesn't help me out when we are screaming at each other, or when we are in an extremely vulnerable place together. It doesn't help the fear or the pain. It doesn't enhance the love that is there. This is entirely my project — mine and Rocky's. That is why marriage and raising a child are such blessings for me. I can't hide inside my money when my daughter falls and hurts herself, or when I take her to the doctor, and she is screaming, and I have to hold her down on the examining table for her shot. Having money doesn't help then. I am still going to feel pain. That is what I want.

I would rather feel any feeling than no feeling. I would rather feel a year's worth of deep, authentic, down-to-my-toes sadness than no feeling at all — which was how I lived most of my life until I was in my late twenties. "Pathetic" doesn't even begin to capture it. It was such a waste. It was so painful.

I want to feel like I'm a member of the human race living on this planet, participating in life. My fear, and what provoked me to go on that bike trip, was my sense that I hadn't been dealt into the game. It's a huge relief to know that I *have* been dealt into the game.

The challenge isn't just for wealthy people — it's for a lot of middle-class people who feel a sense of emptiness. A good portion of Americans have material security — way beyond what people had in the past. The challenge was obvious for people like the pioneers. They had to find a piece of land, clear the trees, plant the fields, and feed their families. That was their sense of purpose. But if that basic stuff is already provided for you, if it takes you a day to buy a house, and you can go to the supermarket for all your provisions, then your existential question becomes, "What is my challenge? How can I connect with authenticity, with significance?"

# Wendy Johnson

*While growing up, Wendy Johnson was presented with two views of wealth: "money is hell," because it created conflict for her father, and "money is power," because her grandmother attempted to blackmail family members with it. As a young adult, Johnson's guilt over her inheritance drove her to prove herself, sometimes in self-destructive ways. Now a therapist, she sees her own behavior around wealth as acting out her family's conflicts. As a mother, Johnson is determined to empower her daughter to live responsibly and confidently with respect to wealth.*

M ost of my money comes from my grandmother, who was the daughter of a pharmacist in the Midwest. She married very glamorous men. She had no ambivalence about money; she loved accumulating it. She was married four times, and she got money from each of her husbands.

Grandmother was disappointed in love at an early age when she learned that her first husband (my mother's father) was having an affair while she was stuck at home with a baby. She was twenty and unprepared for motherhood. Following this, she dedicated herself to leaving the Midwest, seeing the world, and getting rich. She travelled to the Philippines with her second husband's boss and his wife, where she was wined and dined by royalty. When her second husband asked her to stop travelling, she divorced him.

At that point my grandmother came to New York and took up with the café society set. She wanted to live a glamorous high life. She invested the alimony she had received from her first two divorces, and her investments did very well. I think my grandmother saw herself as having earned her money through her wits and charm. She was proud of the fact that she never had a job. In that sense, she may be like the men who amassed fortunes through business and then needed to control what their offspring did with their money. There was a clause in my grandmother's will that forbade any adopted child of mine to inherit any of "her money."

The fact that my grandmother was who she was had a lot of influence on how I saw the money I inherited from her. I have always thought that if my money had come from a more reputable source (some kind of socially useful invention, perhaps), I might feel less conflicted about it. However, I probably absorbed my father's notion that money was so tainted that no source would have felt pure enough.

My mother was neglected by her racy, glamorous mother, who sent her to live in France with relatives for much of her childhood. Having grown up as a "poor little rich girl," my mother was quite conflicted about money. She learned at an early age that money didn't buy the important things, like time, attention, and love. My mother married my father as a rebellion against her mother and her jet-set lifestyle. My father's family was seen as the good, upright, moral family, and my mother's family was seen as the bad, irresponsible family.

My father's money was much more modest. His mother was the daughter of a silversmith, and he came into a small trust at age sixteen when his mother died suddenly during surgery. Some of my father's shame and confusion about money may relate to its coming to him through a tragedy. It was blood money. So it's little wonder that he saw money as the root of all problems. In his late teens, my father lived the high life. He had his own car, and he spent quite a lot of time drinking and carousing. His early inheritance had deprived his own father of any authority over him.

My father was always worried about money. He was in advertising, but he was not a good businessman. The family rumor about my father was that if you gave him $1 million, he would lose it. He couldn't manage money. In fact, there were periods of his life when he was quite impoverished, and I paid his taxes. I think the fact that he was married to a woman who was wealthier than him was tremendously problematic for him. It also drove him crazy that my grandmother had the kind of power she had because she could pay for things. He wasn't sure that he wanted me to go to a boarding school, but he had no say in the decision. He was somewhat castrated by my grandmother's use of her money in the family.

My father had a lot of self-hate around money. I got direct shaming around money from him whenever he was angry at me. He would yell, "You don't know how lucky you are! You're so spoiled! There are so many poor children! I'm going to drive you through Harlem so that you know what life is really like." It was like a fit. He never actually followed through on that threat to drive me through Harlem. My father was very upper class. He'd never been in Harlem in his life except to go to the Apollo Theater to hear some jazz. I subsequently worked in Harlem. All the things that my father threatened he was going to do to me, I did to myself. It was a direct enactment of his conflict because it was in those heightened moments of anger and tension between us that this stuff would come out.

My father used to say, "All of your problems are because you have money." He actually believed that he and my mother had nothing to do with them. I was amazed that he really believed that. He also thought that all the problems between him and my mother were because she had money. He believed that money was the source of all evil, that it ruined his marriages, that it ruined relationships. The irony is that this whole drama was being played out between people of the same class and culture, both of whom had inherited money.

There were two money rules in my family. On my father's side, the rule was: "Hide the money at all costs." And on my grandmother's side, the rule was: "Do what I say at all costs." Or you could put it this way: "Money is hell" and "It's my money."

My mother was caught in the middle between my father and my grandmother. She was just so mixed up about money that she was immobilized. In some ways, she bought my father's whole idea of money as evil, as the source of problems. She couldn't decide whether to ally herself with my father and see her mother as a wicked witch. She was also very dependent on her mother and wanted to please her, but it was hard for my mother to please my grandmother because she was living a suburban housewife's life, and my grandmother's plans had been that she would be a glamorous New York lady. So she rebelled, in a sense, by living in the suburbs. My father didn't treat her very well, so it wasn't the best solution.

When I was ten, my mother took me to New York to see a Broadway show. On the way to the theater, I saw a man with no legs, and he was begging. I gave him all my money and started crying uncontrollably. My mother was furious at me because I was spoiling her day. When we went home, she told my father about it, and he ended up being furious at the beggar, saying he didn't have to go begging in places like that. So there were no clear rules about money in my family. It was a cauldron of confusion.

Because there was so much falseness in the way I was raised, I had no idea that we were wealthy. My parents behaved as if we didn't have money; we didn't live in a fancy way. There was one servant who lived in, but my mother was really my caregiver. She made the beds, she did the laundry, she did the cooking, and she was very involved with me when I was little.

From first to fifth grades, I went to public school. Then I went to a private school, but I still had no idea my schoolmates or my own family had money. People didn't display their money. They were very cautious and guarded about it. It was the old-fashioned hide-your-money, buy-Chevrolets kind of thing. The fact that we had tons of silver just seemed like something that had been passed along. My clothes were second-hand because I was going to outgrow them. I was given an allowance of a dollar a week, and I had a strongbox in which I divided my dollar into nine different compartments. I had a quarter for church and something for school supplies. I actually think my parents did that part rather well: they taught me that if there was something I really wanted, I had to save my money for it. I bought my own radio, I bought my own skis. The only time I got presents was at Christmas and on birthdays.

I remember the first piece of class consciousness I learned was in sixth grade. One day, my teacher, Mr. Jamieson, railed against all of us; he said we were all in the Social Register, we had a lot of money, and we were spoiled. I went home and asked my parents, "What is the Social Register? Are we in it?" It was the first time that somebody outside the family had said, "You are rich." Most of the other children in my class also told their parents what Mr. Jamieson had said, and their parents were outraged. Because I was already primed, my reaction was embarrassment and shame and guilt, but I wasn't sure quite what I was guilty of. I believed that my teacher was right, but my friends said, "He's wrong, we don't have a lot of money." So there was already a difference between how I was seeing the world and how my friends saw it. I didn't seem to have the same sense of entitlement to money that my friends had.

When I was fourteen, I went to a boarding school which I considered to be for dumb, rich girls. And of course, I did not consider myself to be either rich or dumb. I hated that school. I was very unhappy during those teenage years for reasons that didn't have anything to do with money. My parents were getting divorced, and I didn't have any friends. It was a terrible, terrible time in my life. I was internally rebellious and angry, but I didn't act out. Given the possibilities for rebellion, I was a peach. I was on a very bad downhill spiral academically, until I suddenly realized that if I didn't work, I'd have to spend the rest of my life with those dumb, rich girls. That was a huge motive to study.

My parents gave me financial independence at an early age. I had my own clothing allowance at twelve. I used to buy my clothes at Woolworths. I was very surprised, later on, when I went to college and found that other people didn't have checking accounts or allowances. There were girls with rich parents who just gave them money when it was asked for, but not in any way that let them feel a sense of independence. Because I had money, my father gave up all efforts at trying to be a parent, and I was treated like an adult. He assumed I knew what I was doing.

My father also hated the fact that I got money from my grand-mother, and he never let me forget it. My grandmother gave me a car when I graduated from boarding school, even though my father did not want me to have a car. He lobbied hard against it, but he had no choice. So I learned early that money has power and that it's women who have the money *and* the power.

I used to drive all over in my car. I'm lucky I'm alive because I drove very fast. I had been given the weapon of my own destruction. The car my grandmother bought for me was so dangerous, it was recalled the next year. I spun around, and I was in accidents.

One of the many reasons my father didn't want me to have a car was that he didn't want people to know I had money. In his view, if I took the car to Sarah Lawrence, I was going to announce my sense of privilege over other people. He in fact had owned a car when he was in college; he probably had more money than I did at that age because his mother had died when he was sixteen. At Yale in the '30s he must have seemed like a spoiled rich kid. So he was also trying, I think, in a very misguided way, to protect me. But he also seemed to be trying to tell me, "There's something to be ashamed of here, something you should hide, something you shouldn't show. People will see you in a different way, and you will somehow be less valid."

My grandmother insisted that I have a coming-out party. It was dreadful. She also used the fact that she was paying for my college as a bribe to make me go to a particular ball that I didn't want to go to. She was a figure of great proportions because she was so controlling with her money, but it never occurred to her that she'd have a granddaughter she couldn't control.

My conflicts about money and class were so confusing to me that I found all these ways of not letting myself have a good time in society. I would always find a man who had just been kicked out of Princeton or Yale; I found a bad boy wherever I went. I was popular, and I got invited to a lot of coming-out parties, but I turned down most of the invitations. I was turning down a great source of positive reinforcement, turning down a lot of attention, a lot of glamor.

I was very busy trying to get out of my social class. As soon as I went to college, I hid the fact that I had ever been a debutante, and I acted like I didn't have money. I pretended I was on a meager allowance. I was beginning to understand the implications of my class and culture, and I was becoming very involved in the anti-war movement. I decided to drop out of the Social Register. I wrote them a nasty letter, telling them that they were an irrelevant institution and that I didn't want to be associated with the reactionary ranks of American high society. But I didn't tell my parents about that letter; I only told them years afterwards.

My grandmother had been giving me money since birth — $3,000 a year, tax free. I remember her telling me when I was seven that she had been giving me money every year. I was supposed to understand it, but I hated those conversations. By the time I was in college, the investments she had given me were worth about half a million, which yielded an income of $6,000 a year. By New York standards, that's not very much money, but I thought I was a goddamn Rockefeller. I had no sense of proportion.

When my grandmother died, she left me nothing. In fact, she changed her will so that I was not the remainderman because she was afraid that I was going to give my money away or marry somebody of a different religion or color. All my grandmother's money went to my mother. By the time it eventually came to me, it was worth a little over $1 million. For years, I didn't know any of the stocks that I owned; I had never even read my portfolio. It turned out I owned all this Lockheed Aircraft. My grandmother had done a lot of sleazy investing. She was one of those people who's very involved in beating the system in whatever way she could. I told the company that manages my portfolio that I didn't want anything in defense stocks, and they actually listened to me, which was a huge shock. It didn't occur to me that they would really listen. I was a girl — that was how I saw myself at the time — and I had always been treated like I was in some phase that I was going to get over. For a very long time, I was never taken seriously.

After I finished Sarah Lawrence, I met an Argentinian Marxist named Augusto who became my boyfriend. It caused no end of trouble in my Republican, WASP family. My father did something quite smart: he took me out to dinner at a famous restaurant. I was living in a low-income neighborhood, and to go with my father to an elegant restaurant was thrilling for me. By taking me to the restaurant, my father was implicitly saying to me, "This is where you belong — to the manor born — not in some ghetto." He made me feel the contradictions in my relationship with the Marxist. I knew that although I was conflicted about money, I loved the beautiful things that money could buy. I wasn't quite ready to join a revolution.

Then I fell in love with a man named Rick Segal, and we decided to get married. When I told my grandmother I was going to marry Rick, she said, "No you're not! He's Jewish." After I was married, she called his parents and said, "I'm giving Rick and Wendy x amount of money. What are you giving them?" But Rick's parents were not planning to give us anything. Their way of handling money was to provide Rick with an allowance for books and clothes on an as-needed basis. They did not intend to help support us. And Rick was still in school, so I was supporting him.

That was when my conflicts with money really started. I began to see what a mess I had inherited. On the one hand, I was incredibly contemptuous and furious that I was paying for everything, and on the other hand, I was incredibly embarrassed that I had any money at all. I couldn't get it straight whether Rick should be supporting me so that I could be a princess who was taken care of by a wealthy man, or whether I should give away the money and join him on the barricades. I just couldn't position myself.

Rick treated me like I was his parent. I was just there to take care of him and pay the bills and do everything. He was totally impractical, he was totally passive. He acted almost as if he was entitled to be taken care of by me. He had none of my father's guilt about being married to a woman of wealth. All of his income went to his analyst, so he contributed virtually nothing to our household. I was at a loss for words. We had friends whose wives were working to support them, so I felt like I didn't have a leg to stand on.

Rick and I lived on my $6,000 a year, but I thought it was a fortune. I had no sense of what I had because my father had treated me as if I had an enormous amount of money. So much of my view of what I had came from my father's ideas, not from anything objective. Had I wanted things, I could have got a lot more, but the possibility didn't even occur to me. I was trying to live as if I hadn't any money.

Then Rick and I split up, and I hooked up with a man my grandmother really disapproved of. She threatened to disinherit me if I married Harold, but I just said, "You've already given me the money." Harold was just like my father: he both wanted my money and hated me for having it. Unlike Rick, Harold at least had some guilt about being supported, but he didn't think he should work. But I don't think I ever really supported him; we never lived together very coherently. When I moved to Chicago, presumably to be with him, I made sure the lease was in my name, and I paid for everything, so that if I wanted to get out, I could keep the place. So I had learned something about the power of money to give myself independence and safety, but only after having lost a number of apartments. It was a tempestuous relationship.

Harold was working class, and a number of my other boyfriends have also been from the working class. The one I'm most fond of is a man who grew up in Texas. Wayne came from real rural poverty. As a child, he thought he was rich because he had shoes and other kids didn't. He never noticed that he was poor. It's interesting to me, in looking back, that so many of my boyfriends were from working-class backgrounds, although by the time I met them, they had definitely made their way up in the class system. Part of my attraction to men like that was because I too was in the process of changing classes. So I identified with their journey from one class to another. I was denying and hiding my own class origin in the same way that they were denying and hiding theirs. It left me with a feeling of rootlessness, a feeling that I was creating myself. It was a denial of my own history. The occasional time when I did date men from my own class, I held their money against them. But I have never found another culture that I understand as well.

I felt incredibly guilty because I didn't have to work for money. And because I felt so guilty, I worked a lot harder than people who had less money. But the idea that I didn't have to work spoiled it for me. I think the problem with independent wealth is you never feel like you've earned what you get. I'm glad that a work ethic was given to me; it saved my life. But it didn't save me from conflicts around money. Even when I worked for real, people figured out that I had money. I felt guilty because I was part of the problem; I was part of the ruling class; I had gone to a boarding school; I had been a debutante. Most of that stuff I never told anybody, but I knew it.

After working for several years, I went to graduate school to train as a psychotherapist. I continued to work while I was in school. Working was really helping me; I was starting to believe that I was capable. The kinds of comments that I had been so sensitive to, like — "Oh, I'd do that if I had money!" — I began to see how I had let those remarks leave me feeling invalidated. I saw that they were only expressions of other people's jealousy.

I'm trying to explain how my evolution happened because somewhere along the way I became more coherent, less guilt-ridden, and better able to be in charge of my life. At one point my father said to me that he wanted to see my tax return, and I said to him, "It's none of your business." That was the end of his trying to intrude. But it took untold thousands of dollars' worth of psychoanalysis for me to be able to say that to him. It was an expensive comment!

Building my house in Northern Michigan was a turning point for me. I was thirty-one and in graduate school. A piece of land became available that I had been passionate about for years. I remember going to my uncle and asking, like a little girl, "Can I afford to buy this land?" (My mother was alive then, and I still hadn't come into most of my money.) And my uncle said, "My God, you never even bought a watch!" Without him I might have missed that whole opportunity. I bought the land with money I had got from my great-grandfather, who had invested in seeds, and that gave me a certain pleasure. That investment in seeds wasn't like my grandmother's way of getting money, which had been by marrying, getting large chunks of money from each of her husbands, and investing it successfully.

I didn't tell anyone in graduate school that I was building a house, until one day I realized: this is crazy. If I'm going to make new friends, I'm going to have to tell them I'm building a house. So I asked one friend, "Are you going to hate me for doing this?" I literally said that to him! And he said, "No, I might even like you more." His joke helped me realize how crazy I was being about owning my wealth. If someone had helped me recognize what I could have done with my money, I could have been much more helpful to other people, but also much more helpful to myself. I wouldn't have been living in such quasi-phony poverty. Somebody needed to say to me, "You have money. It's a privilege. Don't abuse it."

When my mother died, I inherited more money, which produced in me a desire to live surrounded by beautiful things. I wasn't going to be able to hide my wealth from myself any more. I had received enough extra money that it wasn't just a buffer; I could use it to make a statement. Now I was in charge: both my parents were dead, and I was able to claim the money for myself. I no longer had a parent in my head telling me what to do with my money.

I started to think more coherently about what my money was invested in; I wanted to change the direction of my investments. I took a course in socially responsible investing. I also changed my bank account to the South Shore Bank, which is a socially responsible bank here in Chicago. I changed my Visa card to Working Assets. A few years earlier, I had learned about tithing from a total stranger I was sharing a taxi with. Tithing means that you give away ten percent of your income. I thought that was a great idea, and I tithed for a long time.

Now that I have more money, I don't give away so much of it percentage-wise because I have more expenses, like my daughter Heather's private school. But my pattern of giving has become more conscious. I decided I'm not going to give to anything outside of the U.S. I figure Chicago is a third-world country, and I want to support things in Chicago. Not long ago I was approached by an organization that helps support grass-roots community groups that promote social justice, and we set up a donor-advised fund. I now give them over $1,000 a year in stocks, and I've felt able to get somewhat involved in the organization, which I've never done before. So I'm just beginning to move in that direction, but I'm not up on any barricades.

I think the comfort I feel now has to do with the fact that if I lost my money, I could in fact support myself, and I've never been in that position before. It would be hard if I had to support myself and Heather completely; I'd have to work a lot harder, but I have the credentials and the expertise and the connections to do it. If I didn't know that I could support myself, I think I would feel a little bit like a fraud. I also realize, at last, that I'm very fortunate, and I'm grateful to my grandmother, whom I hated all those years.

I think that a lot of the independence I have is based on having money. Money can give you independence, but it can also give you the illusion of independence. I don't know if I would have had a child on my own if I hadn't had such a substantial nest egg. I think it's real independence, but the money has also made it so that I haven't been forced to work for a living. It has made it easy for me to be in the situation I'm in, and to never need a man to support me. I seem to have developed into a person who finds it very hard to think of letting someone support me, and some of that has to do with money. It's a different form of self-centeredness than you'd normally expect, but there's a kind of fierceness about my independence. Since my marriage to Rick, I've never fallen in love with a man that I've wanted to support. Rick's passivity was very unappealing to me. So my problems in life are more in the interdependent realm — not knowing how to be interdependent with anybody. Somehow the wealth makes it harder for me to work out those issues because I always have an out. I've left millions of men, and it has always been easy for me to leave them. I could just get in my car and leave, knowing that I could pay the rent for a new place.

I want Heather to know a lot more about money than I ever knew, and somehow to present it to her in a way that's not so conflictual. I don't want to make her feel either ashamed, as I did, or entitled. If you feel entitled to money, there's something wrong with you, in my view. But I don't know how I'm going to accomplish that. My tendency is to indulge her. She's only six, and she seems to have the regular greed that all little kids have, but she's not a gimme kid, she doesn't want everything in the store. She can take no for an answer, and she has an intuitively generous spirit; she wants to give away her money to the poor and the homeless. She's already got a social conscience at the age of six. I have conversations with her about spoiling and what's wrong with having everything you want. But she also sees that I treat myself pretty well, that I buy the things I want. She doesn't see me giving money to homeless people. In fact, she criticizes me for not doing it.

So it's very confusing, and it's going to get more confusing when Heather is older because I haven't been rigorous with her in the way my family was rigorous with me, growing up with an allowance that I divided nine different ways. I'm afraid that she's going to make a lot of demands on me for money, and it's going to be very hard for me to say no. And in Chicago, if you give kids money, it increases the likelihood they'll do drugs. I don't know how you do it right with your kids.

*When Wendy Johnson received a transcript of her interview, she responded with a long letter. In it, she spoke about how helpful the interview had been in helping her to clarify her issues with inherited wealth, and she described her recent efforts to take charge of her finances. The following are excerpts from Wendy's letter.*

I have moved more quickly than I expected towards making my portfolio more socially responsible. I now have a second financial advisor whose firm runs checks on companies' records in terms of peace, justice, the environment, animal rights, etc. I make decisions to sell old stocks and buy new ones based on a company's record on how they treat their workers (wages, benefits, working conditions). I have moved money into low-income housing, which yields a tax credit rather than dividends. I have also started a trust fund for Heather. This trust is invested in Working Assets Mutual Funds. My long-range goal is to have all my money invested in companies that I approve of. Since I don't want to spend a lot of time figuring this all out, I am asking the second set of advisors to critique my current holdings.

This represents a reversal of my previous approach. Before, I paid no attention to what my money was invested in, except for the gross parameters like no defense stocks. Eventually, my increased involvement will lead to clashes with my trustees and the money management company (the last vestiges of my family), but I'm not waving any flags. I will make these changes slowly and subtly. It's not a rebellion but an act of appropriation. I have them over a barrel because it is in fact my money, and I pay them to take care of it for me. Until recently — years after my parents and my grandmother had died — I didn't feel like this money was mine. So I had to work through lots of conflicts before I could have even a moderately realistic view of my money. I had to resolve the feeling of being secretly bad and having stolen something from someone I didn't like very much.

I also had to resolve my negative identification with my mother and grandmother and see that, unlike them, I was capable of earning my own way in the world. In short, I had to cast off my father's shame, my mother's confusion and fear of abandonment, and my grandmother's sense of narcissistic entitlement. This took time, psychoanalysis, and real-life changes, like getting a Ph.D., which made me financially independent of my trust. Becoming a mother also helped me feel more entitled to use the money.

For me, owning and using my money is part of a larger pursuit of owning myself. Money had come to represent some bad, illicit part of myself that I had to hide from other people. It was also something that set me apart from other people and made me different. Sometimes this difference propped up a sense of myself as special and entitled (my grandmother's view), but more often, it made me feel less valid, as if my work didn't count as much as other people's work because I didn't have to do it. Furthermore, the money infantilized me and made me feel that I needed it in order to survive. While having money gave me the patina of independence, it tied me to my grandmother and mother in a hostile ambivalence that kept me stuck for years.

Now that some of the mystification has cleared, I see the money simply as something I was born with, like red hair or being female and WASP. Of course, it has created its own set of advantages, but it doesn't by fiat make me any more special or less valid than anyone else. In any culture that both prizes and despises money as much as ours does, it's hard to be even-handed about money.

# Blake Kelly

*By the time Blake Kelly came into his inheritance, his family's business was being artificially maintained at the expense of good financial management. Kelly successfully challenged the trustees' power and drastically influenced the course of his family's wealth. In the process of taking an unpopular stance, however, he alienated himself from some of the staunch traditionalists of his clan.*

I n my family, there is a lot of lore. In the 1870s, there were eight Connells growing up on a farm in Iowa. And down the road, there was another family by the name of Kelly. The Kellys had a similarly large number of children. Two Kelly brothers married two Connell sisters, so the two families almost merged. Then in the next generation, there was another Kelly-Connell marriage, so there were three sources of double cousinage. After that, you had to be careful whom you married.

That entire group of sixteen or so people in the first generation of the Kelly-Connell merger was extremely close. I remember growing up hearing all sorts of stories about these people whom I had never met. Because I knew so much about them, they became for me like people I'd expect would knock on the front door for Sunday dinner.

The money in my family came from T.R. Connell, my great-uncle. He left the family farm and went to law school. Then he practiced debtor-creditor law in North Dakota, which exposed him to a lot of business opportunities. Eventually, he started a power-and-light company, and as a result of the inability of the publisher of the local newspaper to meet a payroll, he also ended up owning a newspaper. Later on, he decided that he was destined for bigger and better things, so in 1890 or so, he took a job with the *New York Times*. He sold the power-and-light company for about $1 million. While this was happening, a senator from North Dakota was talking to his friend, Jim Harris, who owned a large Midwestern newspaper. Harris was bemoaning the fact that the newspaper did nothing but lose money. He asked the senator if he knew anybody who could take a newspaper and make money off of it. The senator said, "There's a young man by the name of T.R. Connell who did that." So they sent my great-uncle a telegram, and word came back that he had left the previous day for New York. Jim Harris thought he might catch T.R. Connell as he was changing trains in Chicago, so he sent a second telegram that said, "Connell, don't go to New York. Come back. Interesting opportunity awaits." That telegram actually reached my great-uncle just as he was changing trains, and he returned to run one of the biggest newspapers in the Midwest.

Before he died in 1918, T.R. Connell did something which was completely and totally uncommon for him: he got into a terrible falling-out with his family over personal matters. He was a flamboyant character, and his own children didn't approve of the way he behaved. So he disinherited his children and left all his wealth to his brothers and sisters. I am descended from one of T.R. Connell's sisters.

There is another part to the story, and that concerns H.L. Kelly. He was my grandfather, brother-in-law to T.R. Connell, and also a lawyer. He had managed to do somewhat the same thing as T.R. Connell had done, and he ended up owning a sawmill in the small town that I grew up in. It evolved into a large agricultural processing company, becoming a $50-million business in the 1960s.

In the old days — and by "old days" I mean the '20s and '30s — all of these businesses kind of operated as family employment agencies. All sixteen of the original Kelly-Connell clan had lots of kids of their own, so when my father's generation was growing up, he and his twenty-five first cousins could just sort of circulate from business to business whenever they needed money. By the time of my generation, there were sixty or seventy mouths around. Everybody had either a real or a next-to-real ownership interest in all the businesses. There was a very misplaced set of priorities on family values versus business values. Despite warnings that should have been heeded, the business was being kept together in a very tightly controlled and manipulative way in order to "foster family interests" that were not really dis-

cernible upon critical investigation. The people who were really bene-
fitting from the business were the people who were actually running
it. And the people who were not running the business hadn't any say.
They wouldn't even have known a newspaper company from a die-
casting operation.

As the family got bigger and bigger, and fewer and fewer people
lived in the upper Midwest, a major sea change occurred. When my
father's generation was running the business, my father and his
twenty-five first cousins all lived within fifty miles of one another. But
in my generation, there is a multitude of cousins. Only half of the
cousins actually know one another, and even fewer live in the
Midwest. So it is a completely different array of people in terms of
their degree of consanguinity and geographic location. All my cousins
are in their fifties and sixties; I am the youngest person in my
generation, and I'm forty-six.

I have always been something of a maverick, and I thought the
business was being artificially held together. So when I joined the
board of directors back in 1983, one of the things I really wanted to do
was to get that on the table as an issue — and I did. I was immediately ostracized by the vast majority of family members. I was
completely and totally excommunicated. And the issue was deemed an
inappropriate subject for conversation. It was just so much a part of
the received wisdom that the company should be preserved as a
family business and controlled by the family, that challenging that idea
meant you must be crazy, demented, and deluded.

Well, the business eventually got sold, but it took ten years. The
family was able to keep the business together for those ten years
because various trusts had been set up which, in essence, vested all the
power in the trustees. The trustees had power not just over the trusts
but also over the assets which the trusts controlled — the businesses.
So a very small group of people was able to have absolute jurisdiction
over those assets without getting input from anybody, if they didn't
want it. And the people who did have that power became extremely
invested in having power. So control was a huge issue — a huge issue.

I viewed it as necessary to get out from under that control because
poor business decisions were being made which were ultimately going
to waste the assets. So I approached the situation by asking: How can

138

we demolish this system of control which is totally debilitating to so many people?

It was a question of education. Starting in the '40s, the company had been changed from an operating company to a holding company, and there was a whole generation of people who basically had no say in the business because it was just an investment business. So a tradition had grown up in that era — from about 1940 to 1976 — that nobody said anything. Nobody even bothered to show up at the shareholders' meetings. Whatever the board of directors thought was the appropriate distribution for that year was what people got, and nobody ever said "Boo." The sub rosa message that everybody was getting was that anything they had to say was: a) not solicited, b) not relevant, c) not wanted, and d) probably wouldn't be listened to. So it took a long time to get people interested in believing that they could say something because the consequences of doing so were fairly Draconian.

By now, most people seem to be happy that the business was sold. I don't know if I am back in everybody's good graces, but I have gotten beyond worrying about it. I don't really care. I have circumscribed greatly the range of relationships that I have within the family. I maintain good, close relationships with the people I really like, and I don't have to have anything to do with those to whom I was artificially bound in the past.

If I were to give advice to others who find themselves in similar situations, it would be: Don't accept the common wisdom. My experience is that the common wisdom comes to the most recent generation for reasons other than their best interests. It has been worked out over many years by people who are substantially older and in very different circumstances than the current generation, for the purpose of perpetuating something that, upon close scrutiny, might or might not be worthy of perpetuation.

The received wisdom is an enormous monolith that needs to be dealt with. And because there are so many people who are invested in the received wisdom, it is a daunting task to try either to challenge it or to change it. But if you do not try to challenge it or change it, you will lead a life of passivity. If you want to do that, that's fine. Your challenge in life then becomes much more circumspect, and your question becomes: How do I lead a life that is not one of self-centeredness?

If you are really interested in having an active life, you are going to have to challenge the common wisdom. And if you actually undertake that as the road you would prefer to follow, you are going to have to distance yourself and free yourself to pursue whatever it is that you want to pursue in a productive way. Until you come to grips with the monolith, it is a bit like being under the sway of Hal, the giant computer in the Kubrick movie, *2001*. The monolith is going to control you and everything you do — your personal relationships and your whole approach to life. And it will, in fact, relegate you to passivity and probably to some sort of solipsistic eccentricity.

# Rachel Halpern

*When she was fifteen, Rachel Halpern's father died, leaving her $6 million as well as his home and his Mercedes. Suddenly Halpern had to deal with the power and responsibilities of an adult. In college, she developed a keen sense of social activism and took pleasure in using her resources for community-based housing and gardening projects. Yet she fears the subtle and not-so-subtle resentment of her peers. She often wonders how she can reconcile her inheritance with her commitment to social activism.*

Neither of my parents had money when I was little. My dad's father died when Dad was fourteen, and before he died, he told my dad, "Take care of your mother and your sister." And my dad set out to do exactly that. He worked at every odd job he could find — from the post office to the check-out line at the grocery store — and he managed to support his mom and his sister. Then he went to California, and he pretty much did everything he could to make money. When my mom met my dad, he was setting up a huge office with a desk that flipped around into a liquor cabinet. It was raised up like a throne. And Mom said, "What is this office for?" I don't think he had any idea what it was for; he just wanted to be a businessman. His partners still laugh today about the things they did to make extra profit when they started building apartments. They used to build them with half the number of nails that were required.

When my dad and his partner started their business, it was just the two of them. By the time he died, he had about sixty people working for him. He turned into one of the biggest developers in Los Angeles. I think he invented the concept of the mini-mall. It's sometimes called the "pod mall," and a lot of developers copied him.

My mom and dad got divorced when I was two. Mom and I moved into a little tiny apartment, and Dad lived in a small house. Then he started getting more and more money, and while we still lived in our small apartment, he built a larger house. So there were discrepancies as I was growing up. My mom was the one who provided the little essential things, like making my lunch and giving me kisses, and my dad provided the big financial things.

I didn't quite know what my dad did for a living, and I was always confused about it. I would ask him, "Daddy, what *are* you?" and he'd say, "I'm a developer." But I didn't know what a developer was, so I'd ask him again, and he'd say, "I'm an entrepreneur." But I didn't know what that meant, either. From early on, he taught me a few essential lessons. One of them was the meaning of profit, and I was like a little piece of entertainment for him at parties. He'd say, "Rachel, what is profit?" And I'd say, "Profit is the difference between the cost and what you sell it for," and all his friends would laugh.

I asked him once if he was rich, and he told me that he wasn't rich, he was comfortable. He definitely joked about it. And I think since he'd grown up not having anything, getting rich was a real joy for him.

I started having more of the privileges of money in my early teens. My dad and I would go on sailing trips, and he took me to Italy. I also had certain bizarre privileges. Dad was a patron for the '84 Olympics, so I ran in the Torch Relay. I had no idea why I was doing it. He was always pushing me to the forefront. He tried to get me to go to private school for a long time, but I kept saying, "No, I want to be with my friends." Finally, I went to a private day school in Los Angeles. It was a relaxed school where you didn't have to wear shoes, and it was a lot of fun and a great school. It was an enclave for rich kids, and there were a lot of children of famous people. The school definitely had its fair share of BMWs. L.A. is so car-centric. We used our cars for lockers, and we'd sit on them in the parking lot and socialize. Who you were was defined by what kind of car you had. I had a jeep, which had the benefit of being hip and not too snotty. My father had a Mercedes, and sometimes I'd have the Mercedes because he wanted to drive the jeep. I remember thinking, "Oh, God, I'll be so embarrassed to drive that Mercedes!" Even then I thought it wasn't cool to flaunt your wealth.

My dad died after heart surgery when I was in tenth grade. Stress killed him. He worked all the time; it was a crazy way to live. I learned a lot about how not to live from watching him. Because he died so suddenly, there was no time for me to prepare for his loss.

It took the lawyers five years to work out my dad's estate. It was difficult for me to deal with because I had to be in front of so many lawyers in so many mahogany-tabled conference rooms. It was upsetting because no one my age understood my experience. I wasn't able to talk to anyone about my father's death.

I'm the primary beneficiary in my father's will. I was heir to all his personal possessions. It was weird to be fifteen and have a big house and a Mercedes. I had no way of dealing with it. I hung on to the house for a while. I remember my dad's partner saying, "The maintenance on this house is costing you as much as buying a new BMW every month and driving it off a cliff."

After Dad died, I went right back to school and pretended that nothing had happened. I didn't care about the money; I just wanted my father. People were telling me, "You don't need to work," but I didn't give a shit. My mom told me that I had the opportunity to do whatever I wanted, that I didn't have to worry about making money. She was coming from having to work for fifteen years as a legal secretary. But other people were saying, "You're rich! Isn't that exciting?" That's just what I didn't want to hear. I remember saying to someone right after my dad died, "I don't care that I have a house and a car and a million dollars. I miss my father." I obviously said it to the wrong person because it got around the school, and people were saying, "Oh, you have a million dollars!" It was depressing because my point was not at all about the money, but that was what got around.

I began to hate the money. I felt like it was a bad thing in my life. I signed where the lawyers said, "Sign," but I wouldn't touch the money. Now, eight years later — I'm twenty-three — I'm starting to be more adjusted to it, and I'm happy that I'm able to do these things in my life that feel great.

I went to Reed College. Unlike many colleges, it's not cool to be wealthy at Reed. A lot of kids would wear ripped-up jeans and bandanas on their heads. They looked like street bums, but they drove

BMWs and Saabs. I completely hid my wealth. I was so concerned that someone would find out I had money, and I didn't know how to deal with it or tell my friends. I remember somebody calling me a rich bitch behind my back. I thought: I'm not the sort of person who would be called a bitch, so it must be something about my wealth. But how would they know? I didn't have many possessions, and I was shocked that someone had found out, as if it was a big secret.

I decided that I wanted to study architecture. Since my father was a developer, I had developed a passion for buildings. He took me to a lot of building sites when I was little, and I would go into these stick-frame things and look around and say, "That must be the bathroom, and that must be the bedroom." It's ironic because he developed Los Angeles, and I don't want to develop anything. I think I may exist to tear down what he built. For years, I've been involved in the movement toward social and environmental change.

I started working part-time as a volunteer for a community land trust. It was one of my first direct connections with an underprivileged community, and it was an amazing experience. It connected me with a lot of things that I wouldn't have seen otherwise, and it put a different slant on my plans. I was having to to deal with social issues, which are the real issues. I already knew that I didn't want to be an architect for rich people. In school, all they teach you is how to design pretty houses and office buildings for rich people. There wasn't any class I could take that would teach me how to work with low-income people.

Working for the land trust led me toward thinking about money and the discrepancies between rich and poor, and how scary those discrepancies are. I started to feel like I could made a personal contribution. And I started to realize that through the work I wanted to do and with the money I had, I could make a difference.

Then I got another half-time job, working at an organic market garden. I didn't tell the farm people that I wasn't getting paid at the land trust because I didn't want them to question how I could make ends meet on my stipend of forty dollars a week. I got direct questions all the time like, "How can you afford that?" One day, someone noticed the ring my father had given me and said, "God! that must have been expensive!" There was no way for me to answer comments like that. What could I say? "Oh, I'm really rich, you know."

*Rachel Halpern*

Volunteer work was starting to feel thankless. After I had been working at the land trust for a year, we had an annual meeting, and everyone was thanked but me. I went home and cried. Then I thought, "This is bullshit. Why am I crying?" The next day I went in and told the director, "If someone works for you for free, twenty hours a week, you need to give them something back. You need to stand up and say, 'I'd like to acknowledge this person.'" I'm glad I had that experience. I learned a lot about what I need.

I realized one day that I needed either to quit or to ask for pay. Being a volunteer wasn't doing it for me. I was starting to think that I needed to be paid what I was worth, but I didn't need any more money. I grappled with those questions all by myself; I didn't know anyone who could understand what I was talking about. And then I realized what "need" means to me, and that it doesn't mean that I need money to buy bread. It means I need money for my self-esteem. I told my boss that if I were to continue my work, I wanted to get paid. It was the biggest deal for me to ask him, and he just said okay. He said he'd pay me fifteen dollars an hour, which was more than I would have asked for. I was waiting for five bucks an hour, and he was paying me a hundred dollars a day! It was a big victory for me.

After I graduated from college, I moved to New England and started working — as a volunteer — with an organization called Jardines del Pueblo, which means "the people's garden" in Spanish. Jardines del Pueblo is an organization that promotes community and economic development through urban agriculture. We have a community garden with almost forty plots, and we're starting a food co-op. That was my fantasy in college, but I didn't think it could actually happen. And now we're talking about developing an education program. It's an amazing organization! I'm in love with the work.

There's this guy I work with, José, and he is fifty-something. He said to me one day, "I've worked every day of my life, and I'll never make enough money to have the car you have." We were standing next to my beat-up old Jeep, and it made me sad that this man would never be able to afford what, in my mind, was a beat-up old car. It made me sad too that he thought my car was something amazing.

145

My money is in three trusts, and the main trust is irrevocable. I'll get distributions when I'm twenty-five, thirty, and thirty-five. I'm not at all uncomfortable with the degree of control that I have over my money because I feel like the money is being handled in a way that I can deal with. My accountant is always saying, "I got a check. Do you want it, or shall I deposit it?" and I've always told her to deposit it. But the last time, I took the money. It was a relatively small amount — $35,000. I decided that I would experiment with it; I would give away half and invest half. So far, I've given away half, but I haven't invested the other half yet. I'm a lot better at giving my money away than I am at keeping it. I thought it was auspicious that I'm starting this money work now because when I'm twenty-five, I'm going to get more money, and I need to do something good with it. I think two years will give me enough time to figure out what I want to do. I'll probably keep practicing.

After that, I began to develop my personal giving philosophy. I decided to give to places that shared my beliefs in grassroots, sustainable change, and to give back to places that had given to me. I gave a large chunk of my practice money to an organization in California that I had worked with when I lived out there. The person who runs the organization is someone I love and respect, and I gave him money for a book he's writing. I also gave to Reed College to help start an urban gardening project in Portland. Another part of forming my ideas about giving has been learning how to say no. I'm learning to be clear about what I want kinds of causes to give money to, so that when someone calls me to ask for a donation or when I get something in the mail, I'll be able to say, "That's not part of my personal giving philosophy."

My investment portfolio is really ugly — Pepsi, General Motors, Philip Morris — all sorts of big nasties. I wrote a letter to the people managing the estate, saying that I wanted to have more socially and ecologically responsible investments. They of course gave me a big rap about what's profitable. That's their bottom line. All of them — my lawyer, my accountant, and my executor — say, "We want to work in your best interest." "Your best interest" to them is maximum profit, but my best interest, to me, is *not* maximum profit. So we butt heads, but I think they know how I feel. They're not scary people, and I love them. It helps that I love them. We just have different ways of looking at the world. It's been difficult to get my investment advisors to switch over any of the stocks. They've sold a few, and they've bought a few more, but they're definitely not thinking like I am.

I understand that they've been raised to think that way. My mom didn't raise me like that at all; she just didn't care much about money. So I have the benefit of having grown up with different values. It's partly a generational thing and partly a gender thing. I'm finding that many people of my generation — especially women — have the attitude that their wealth and their other resources are things to be shared.

I started researching socially responsible investment advisors, and I saw an ad for the Impact Project. The directors of the Impact Project, Anne Slepian and Christopher Mogil, sent me some information, and it looked great, so I set up a meeting with them. We dealt with some big questions in our first meeting. One question was how much money I actually had, and I realized that I didn't know. I thought I had about $2 million. We added up my assets. The funny thing was that I could have done it on my own, but I never had. We added up how much was in each of the trusts, the value of the house I bought for my mother, what I had in my account, and what my accountant had in her accounts. And it added up to $6 million! It really, really, really blew me away. If I had thought about it, I would have realized that the house alone was worth over $1 million. We also talked about other stuff, like what I wanted to do with my life, issues of work, and issues of relationship. After that meeting, I came home to Luke, who's my sweetie, and I told him how much money I had. He comes from a middle-class family, and he was as blown away as I was.

I was still working for Jardines del Pueblo, the urban gardening project. At first, we were all working together, doing the same amount of work, and no one was getting paid. Finally the organization received a small grant, and I was asked to be the staff person. I started getting eight dollars an hour for twenty hours a week, but I was working a lot more hours than that. The organization was struggling. I had a meeting with Christopher and Anne at the Impact Project, and I told them that I didn't know what to do. I could have funded Jardines del Pueblo myself, but that wouldn't have helped me, and it wouldn't have helped the organization to become self-sustaining. We didn't even have money to buy stamps. I was spending ten hours a week trying to write little grant proposals for $500 for office supplies, and it was a waste of my time. Anne and Christopher helped me decide to make a small grant of $500 for office supplies. So I told a board member whom I trust that I had been given some money by a family member, and I wanted to give it to Jardines del Pueblo. She thought that was great, and she told me we could keep it anonymous. It was really liberating for me. I got myself out of my personal difficulty of figuring out how to pay for stamps and stationery, but I didn't do the organization a disservice. Now I'm dealing with the question of whether to give a more substantial amount of money to Jardines del Pueblo because we don't have any money left. I'd be basically paying my own salary.

Three months ago, I started keeping a budget and tracking everything I spent. I wanted to figure out how much I needed to live on, and I wanted to see if my job was paying for it. It was an interesting exercise. I know I can live without certain things. I live modestly, and that's a conscious choice. I pick my luxuries, like travel, since my family lives on the West Coast. Hearing people tell me "You don't need to work" frustrates me. I want to work, and I want to know that I can be financially independent. As a woman, it's a strength I want to have.

I'm still scared to tell people at Jardines del Pueblo about my money. I'm afraid of what they'll think. I've seen how critical people are of the rich, how condemning. And I want to show people that there's someone with money who is not the way they think. It's important to break down these stereotypes about people with money, but at the same time, I'm scared to reveal my wealth. I think I'm going to leave this job without telling my co-workers. But before long, I'm going to have to confront my fears. Having to hide is sick; it's weird. I didn't choose this life; I didn't do anything wrong. I got the money, and I'm doing such good things with it. I want to be able to inspire others.

# Chuck Collins

*Chuck Collins gave away his inheritance of $300,000 when he was twenty-six. He has gone public a number of times to talk about why he gave his wealth away, and to encourage other heirs to follow his example. He has successfully integrated his political philosophy with his financial way of life and enjoys a deep involvement in his community.*

M y father, whom I love and respect, has told me, "You know, you really ought to stop talking about this because you've crossed the line into a certain level of egotism." He believes that the gift given anonymously is the most powerful gift, the gift where you are not going to get credit, or you're not going to get anything back, or you're not going to have your name on the side of a building. I told my father that I'm just trying to make it possible for other rich people to see that there is a life beyond privilege, and I tell my story because I hope it will change society.

I grew up in an affluent suburb of Detroit — Bloomfield Hills, Michigan. We lived in an unpretentious old farmhouse with a barn and a couple of acres of land to play in. It was a great place. I went to private schools with people like Cathy Iacocca and other children of captains of industry. We were members of a country club, but I always thought we were upper-middle class because there were people in Bloomfield Hills who were a lot richer and more ostentatious than we were. I'm not alone in America in being confused about class.

The money I inherited came down to me from Oscar Mayer, the meat packer — a household name in America. He was my great-grandfather on my father's side. He started a butcher shop in Chicago at the turn of the century. My father had very little involvement with the company; he went off and worked for twenty-five years for another company. Then he decided to do other things with his life: he went to art school, he and my stepmother renovated and operated an inn, and he started a land conservancy organization. He really has followed his passions. At the same time, he has always worked hard and not always for money.

Both my parents are good role models. My mother has an incredible sense of fairness. She taught us not to hurt people, to respond to other people's suffering, and to take responsibility for each other. I would characterize my father as a conservative economic libertarian. He voted for Reagan and Bush, and he believes that government should get the heck out of the economy. His views are thoughtful and historically rooted in his own experience. I always enjoy engaging with my father around politics. I have a lot in common with him: we are both extremists. There's a picture of my father and me in my hall: He is holding up the *National Review*, William F. Buckley's magazine, and I'm holding up the *Radical American*. The caption under the picture is "Extremism runs in the Collins Family."

I believe in individual responsibility, and my father does too. He used to say, "Don't sit back and complain; do something about it." He is a doer. That is a legacy from both my parents. Both my father and I believe that it's not a good idea to look to government to solve all the problems that individuals are responsible for. We are also strong environmentalists. Where we differ, I think, is that my experience working in low-income communities here and in Central America has shown me that the playing field is not level. The odds are stacked against low-income people, and the rules are set up to benefit people who already have vast concentrations of wealth. I was taught the golden rule: "Do to your neighbors as you would like to be treated by them," but over time I have learned the "real" golden rule: "The people who have the gold make the rules."

All of us kids were brought up with the expectation that we would work. Our parents' message was: contribute somehow to the common good. When we were in our teens, we had jobs. We had to do something, but it didn't have to be paid work. We could volunteer to teach swimming, or whatever. Very early on I started a little business trimming hedges and mowing grass for my neighbors. Later I worked as a caddy at a golf course or washed dishes. I have a long dishwashing resumé.

When I was sixteen, my father told me, "You are going to inherit money. You will not have to work if you don't want to, but I hope you will work and have a meaningful life. Please don't let this inheritance be a hindrance; use it as a tool to get the education you want, and to give yourself opportunities in terms of your own path." Suddenly I realized, "Oh! This isn't just about growing up in Bloomfield Hills and having a nice house. This is going to affect me in a big way. I'm going to have a pile of money to deal with." I had definitely been bumped up to another category. It wasn't just that my parents were rich; *I* was rich, and I was different.

It felt like a mixed blessing from the start. I didn't want anyone to call me a rich person. I didn't even want anyone to know! I didn't want my wealth to affect my friendships. And I was already conscious that there was something wrong with the way wealth is distributed. Growing up in Detroit in the sixties, it was hard to miss seeing that something was wrong. I was eight when the Detroit riots broke out, and I was fascinated by those riots. I clipped articles out of *Life Magazine* and kept them in a scrapbook. I have vivid memories from TV of National Guard tanks rolling down the streets and buildings burning. I don't think I got a whole lot of help understanding what was happening, but that's when the simmering began in me. Something inside kept saying, "This is wrong, this is wrong, this is wrong." It didn't make sense that some people have so much and most have so little. At different times in my life, that simmering has been turned up to a boil.

When I was eighteen, I went to Worcester, Massachusetts, to work in an internship program called Dynamy. I was reluctant to go to college without some more concrete work experience. Over the course of the year, I did several internships, including teaching in an early childhood center. The experience that affected me the most was working as a community organizer — registering voters and organizing tenants in public housing.

I did that internship because I had a hunger to get real, to understand the world, and to get out of the pretense bubble I had grown up in. Living in Worcester, which is a working-class city, I was thrown out of my class milieu into a very different class background. It was a good experience — living in a city instead of the suburbs and getting to know people who were different from me because they had grown up poor. Some of my own class attitudes got confronted. I felt a sense of shame about my origins, so I would just be silent and listen to everybody else tell their stories, but I would not tell mine. I was trying to obscure the fact that I was upper class and rich. My unacknowledged wealth was adding a layer of shame whenever I engaged with the world.

It was impossible for me to ignore certain things. At most points where I've had the choice either to plunge in and take risks and confront class issues, or try to stay safe. More often than not, I've leaned towards the more difficult road. It felt like I had a lot to learn.

The first time I went to a conference for people with inherited wealth, I was eighteen. It was 1979 in Boston, and the conference was organized by the Haymarket People's Fund. Haymarket was one of the early social change foundations. It was started by progressive donors like George Pillsbury, who was heir to the flour fortune. Haymarket's founders had a commitment to funding "change, not charity." Going to that conference was a revelation! These were my people! I didn't know that anyone else from my social background had the same views of the world that I was wrestling with. Wealth conferences allow you to see that you're not alone. You also need to build ongoing relationships; attending a conference once a year is not enough. I came of age with the help of Haymarket People's Fund. I was very lucky. I tremble at the thought of what my life would have been like if I hadn't been able to plug into that network. I haven't done any of this work alone; it has all been together with other people.

Four years later, I was at another Haymarket People's Fund wealth conference, and we were playing the up-and-down-the-mountain game. Do you know that game? Everyone stands in a big circle, and someone — it could be anyone — walks into the center of the circle and says, "Who had grandparents who lived in a mansion?" and all the other people whose grandparents lived in mansions go into the center. We were playing that game, and somebody said, "Who thinks about giving away their assets? " Five of us jumped into the middle of the circle. We decided to have lunch together, and from there we formed a support group. Four of us continued to meet for four years. And out of that, we took action that changed our lives.

Edorah Frazer and Christopher Mogil were also in that little group. We prepared carefully: We planned out where to give our money and how to communicate with our families. We also helped each other think through the "what if" questions. I had started getting income from my trust when I was in college, and I knew that I would get control of the whole kit and caboodle at twenty-six. Edorah gave away eighty percent of her inheritance, and I gave away all of mine — $300,000. I gave the money to the Funding Exchange to set up a donor-advised fund, and I allocated it immediately to the Haymarket People's Fund, the Fund for Southern Communities, and the Peace Development Fund.

Christopher Mogil took a somewhat different tack. He decided to experiment with sharing decision-making about funding with a group of fellow activists. There's no single right way to do any of this. I have one path, and Christopher has another.

Giving the money away was part of a whole process of coming to terms with my legacy. It wasn't just an act of rejection; it was part of a process of learning to believe that I didn't really need the money, that I was going to be okay, and that I was going to be able to provide for myself. I wanted to make a choice that would align my values and beliefs with my actions.

I had been involved in solidarity work in Central America. In Nicaragua, I'd worked on the cotton and coffee harvests, and I had worked in a refugee camp in El Salvador. So I had been doing things in my life to try to rectify the gross inequalities in society, but when you are sitting on a mountain of money, *you* become part of the problem. I was in the top one percent of the population who own thirty-seven percent of all the wealth. I believe that the root cause of our social and political problems is the great concentration of wealth in the hands of so few people. I have faith that we are a wealthy planet, that there's enough to go around, and that nobody needs to go hungry. The choice to share my wealth, to return it to others, is part of my path of clearing out the things in my life that have prevented me from looking people in the eye. For me to keep holding onto my wealth would have amounted to living a lie. My unacknowledged wealth was adding a layer of shame whenever I engaged with the world. It was interfering with all my relationships. Having money actually blocks you from getting help from other people. Instead of asking your friends to help you move into your new apartment, you pay someone to help you. My path is to recognize and honor my interdependence with all human beings, and I understood that my money was only going to confuse that.

Even now I don't feel like I'm a working-class person. I'm still a person of privilege, even though I no longer have the money or access to any other money. I continue to live with the nonmoney privileges of my upbringing. It was a privilege even to be able to decide to give my money away. I still have good relationships with my family; I'm not going to go wanting.

At the time I gave the money away, I was working at the Institute for Community Economics in Greenfield, Massachusetts. The mandate of ICE, as we call it, is to provide assistance and financing to community-based affordable housing and business development. I worked in the field program, assisting organizations to start community loan funds and community land trusts for affordable housing.

It was through ICE that I had exposure to a whole other world of possibilities, and I was able to see a lot of constructive changes happening. I think some people hold on to their money because they don't believe that any good can come out of giving it away. But that's a cynical view about the possibilities for change. At ICE I was constantly being exposed to great community development projects and excellent grassroots organizing. So it was easy for me to see that my money could immediately change situations, that it could radically alter the face of a neighborhood.

I could look back on my decision to give away my inheritance and say, "Well, geez, did I have to give it *all* away? Why did I have to do that?" It just seemed like it was the right thing to do at that particular time, and the consequences are that I have to earn a living and save money like everyone else I know. I don't have any regrets. I'm thankful for every opportunity I've had — the opportunity to grow up without want, the opportunity to confront having the money, the opportunity to make the decision to give it away, and the path that giving the money away has led me down. I've had to think about how to earn money, how to budget, how to get control over the economic realm of my life. If I want to have children — which I do — and a house with a few blades of grass that they can run around in, I have to figure out how to support them. I have also made a choice to pursue my basic needs in a more collective manner, as opposed to just having my own individual mountain of money. So when my children are old enough for school, I won't be able to opt out of the public school system and simply buy their way into a private school. If I want them to have a decent education, I will have to fight for the improvement of the public school system. I've seen the effects of individual solutions to community problems, like sending children to private schools. It's not good that the wealthiest ten percent of the country have privatized their basic needs. It has meant that they've withdrawn their support from the important community institutions that sustain everyone else, whether it's a library or a public transit system. To me, the essence of privilege and entitlement is the image of the rich man in the middle of a traffic jam saying, "I shouldn't have to sit here in this traffic jam. This is for the common people. I should just be able to levitate outta here."

Over a year ago, I left the Institute for Community Economics to become the director of a statewide coalition of affordable housing groups in Massachusetts. We are working to change the state's budget priorities so that lifeline programs for low-income people don't get cut away. We define "success" as keeping lifeline social programs from being slashed as fast as they would have been if we weren't there.

I feel like I'm on the verge of what might become my life's work. I've been thinking about how to organize to build a movement that would actually shift the balance of power, that would change the rules of the tax code, because it really comes down to that. The eighties was a period of increasing concentration of wealth, and certain changes in the tax rules contributed mightily to making the rich richer, and the poor poorer. In 1975, the top one percent of income holders, of which I was a part, owned nineteen percent of all the wealth in the United States. And today in 1993, the top one percent owns thirty-seven percent of all the wealth. So the top one percent picked up one percent a year of the nation's wealth for eighteen years. That wouldn't be so bad if it didn't also mean that the bottom ninety percent lost a fairly significant chunk of their wealth. And there are a lot of people in the middle of that ninety percent — the traditional middle class — who are feeling very precarious.

I've been studying American history. During the 1880s and '90s, there were social movements that played a significant role shifting the distribution of wealth and power in the United States. These movements pushed for what eventually became the first income taxes. And during the 1930s, Huey Long in Louisiana, a seamy but interesting character, founded the Share-the-Wealth Movement. Seven million people joined Share-the-Wealth Societies all over the country; they essentially pushed Roosevelt to legislate progressive taxation. So there are some examples of people actually organizing to change the rules.

Tax rules subsidize the wealthy to an incredible degree. Because I work in housing, I'm aware of the Home Mortgage Interest Deduction. It allows people to deduct the interest on their mortgage from their income tax. And of course, the bigger your house and the more houses you own, the bigger your mortgage will be and the more interest you can deduct from your taxes. The Home Mortgage Interest Deduction is essentially a mansion subsidy. Forty billion dollars a year of revenue doesn't come in to the government coffers because people with mega-houses can deduct their mortgage interest. That's more than twice as much money as the federal government spends on low-income housing. So the biggest housing subsidy goes to the very wealthy.

I'm working with a crew of around forty people who are looking at ways to design a 1990s Share-The-Wealth movement. We are starting with a simple stage-one campaign platform: we will be asking government to eliminate subsidies for the wealthy. The second-stage campaign will be to push for progressive capital gains taxation and other forms of wealth taxation. We want to create local Share-The-Wealth clubs just like in the old days. We plan to go around and talk to people about these issues. Our idea is that the local Share-The-Wealth clubs would organize to hold legislators accountable in ways that they are not now accountable. We're about to fund-raise and hire staff for the first phase of the project.

I think there's an important role for wealthy people in our movement for economic justice because wealthy people are authorities on the problems of privilege. They understand that privilege doesn't solve all your problems, and they have a front-row seat on how the system works to benefit them unfairly. There's a whole cadre of wealthy people who are willing to go public and talk about all the subsidies they get, and how it's not fair, and it's not a good use of taxpayers' money to subsidize the rich. It's important for members of the owning class to speak out: speaking out legitimizes the aspirations of people who don't have wealth.

On the other hand, a movement for economic justice is really about people without wealth reclaiming their power. As wealthy people, we can talk about charity, we can talk about giving away our money for the homeless in our streets, but the reality is that the money does not belong to us. It is not our legitimate claim. We don't have any claim on all that value that has accumulated on our side of the ledger.

People from the owning class can also support the movement for social justice through funding organizations like the Haymarket People's Fund. Haymarket funnels money directly to groups that are trying to reclaim power for ordinary people. The movement for social justice is ultimately about those people organizing to change the rules in order to reclaim the government which has been taken away from them — reclaim the United States Senate from the millionaires. Why can't there be plumbers and McDonald's employees in the senate?

# Patricia Taylor

*Throughout Patricia Taylor's childhood, which included summers in fashionable Newport, wealth meant position, isolation, and denial. As a young adult, Taylor began to identify the hidden drug and alcohol abuse that drove the emotional undercurrents in her family. Spurred by a sense of emptiness and longing, Taylor embarked on a remarkable journey which healed her isolation and nourished her spiritual life. She is now deeply connected to the world through her Christian faith and her genuine ability to care for herself and others.*

How rich is my family? When I was preparing for this interview, I asked my younger sister some of your interview questions. One of those questions was: "Do you feel rich?" And her answer was, "Oh, no, no. I'm comfortable." So I asked her, "Who is rich, then?" and she said, "Well, Annie [another sister] is rich." So I said, "Oh, okay. Now I know." [Laughs.] Then I asked Annie, "Do you feel rich?" and she said, "Oh, no, I'm comfortable. I've always felt that I'm in the middle." In the context of our family history, you could manage to be "in the middle" when you had the Buckleys and the Duponts living nearby. It all depends on your frame of reference. And I am laughing because I am like that, too. There is a part of me that wants to say, "No, I'm not rich. I'm comfortable." Mother used to say, "There's rich, and then there's rich rich." There was always somebody above you. It's the prize, but no one wants to wear the blue ribbon.

Both my parents and my grandparents on both sides came from wealthy families, and the money goes back for quite a few generations. On my father's side a lot of the money was from Bethlehem Steel and First National City Bank. So both my parents were born into a very gilded world. My mother spent every summer of her whole life in Newport.

My father always seemed to have a difficult time making peace with money. He was a bright, competent, passionate man, and I think he was overwhelmed by the situation he lived in. He married an English girl, a Catholic, which was a no-no, and his father disinherited him. Later on, his father was sick, and my father gave his own blood for a transfusion. It's such a painful image: there they were, side by side, the disinherited son giving blood to the father. So there's a painful legacy in my family around inherited wealth because you could be disinherited. In fact, both my father and my stepfather were disinherited. The sons were not given the fathers' blessings. How difficult it is to go out into the world when you do not have the blessing of the father! It's such a burden, such a wound. My mother remembers my cousin asking, "How many times have you been disinherited?"

My mother met my father in Newport at a debutante party that he was giving for his stepdaughter. Mother was twenty-two, and he was sixteen years older. He had already been married twice. They bought a farm in Seakonk, Massachusetts, and that's where my sisters and I lived until I was six.

We had a nanny, whom we called Nanny. Nanny was essential. She was an English nanny without the whimsy of Mary Poppins. It's funny — my oldest sister and I were later in therapy groups, and we used to ask each other, "Have you told them about Nanny yet?" And I would say, "Oh, no." You could speak about anything, but to speak about Nanny was to tell about the dirtiest secret. My older sister and I experienced our history in similar ways; we did a lot more struggling than my younger sisters ever did with wealth and guilt, and what the wealth meant in our lives. And Nanny was central in that because Nanny was what made us different. She represented not being brought up by your mother, but being brought up by a servant. Just the fact of having a nanny separated us, especially after we moved to South Carolina, but not in Newport; everybody had nannies in Newport.

On the other hand, Nanny was a central, loving figure for me. She was somebody that I was ashamed of, and I was ashamed of being ashamed of her because I loved her, too. Nanny was always there, from the time we got up in the morning until we went to bed at night. And if we woke up in the middle of the night, Nanny was there. Our days were very structured, according to the British way — very formal. We got up at 7:15; not at 7:30. We had breakfast at 7:30, we had lunch at 12:30, and then we had a walk. Everything went according to clockwork. And we all dressed alike. Nanny wore a white uniform that had special buttons. I'd play with them while she brushed my hair. She had white stockings and white shoes.

We traveled in a clump. We were like a club — "the girls." We felt like we were a central force in the family because our fathers changed several times. My father was married five times, my first stepfather was married five times, my second stepfather was married three times, and my mother was married three times. Altogether there were sixteen children in the extended family — four sisters, ten stepsisters, and two stepbrothers. My sisters and I were the part that didn't change, and Nanny too, because Nanny always went along.

Nanny was also the one who passed along a lot of the rules about money. She was the communicator of values in the household. My parents didn't talk about money, and there wasn't a lot of talk about divorce. Much later, my mother said that she was always trying to protect us from things. But Nanny felt no such compunction. Nanny would give her own view, sometimes quite incorrect, but certainly her view, of what was going on. She'd do this by telling us stories that we thought were the truth. She also sang us songs. I remember one that began: "I once had a beautiful doll, dear," and she would go on and on about how she'd lost her beautiful doll, dear, and the snows came. Then in the springtime she found her doll, dear, but it was all tattered and torn. But she loved this doll, anyway. The moral of the story was that Nanny only had one doll, but she appreciated it and loved it. And we had lots of toys, unlimited amounts of toys, but we did not appreciate what we had. We were spoiled.

Nanny would tell us stories about her family, whom I knew more about in many ways than my father's family. My father rarely talked about his brothers and sisters. But I heard all about Nanny's mother and father and her brother John and her sister Violet. They didn't have a lot, but they loved each other, you know. This was a constant commentary. And when I was six, and my parents were getting divorced because of another woman, Nanny would say things like,

"Shh, don't bother your mother." And then she'd say in a hushed voice, "He's broken her heart," and she'd make clucking noises and say, "Too much money." So money was the cause of the divorce as well as the cause of unhappiness, the reason families weren't together. If there wasn't a great deal of love in the family, money was the cause. "Too much money," she would say.

That was one part of Nanny's message. There was also a certain snobbish quality in Nanny: she was pleased about the wealth. When we were in Newport, we would go to birthday parties several times a week, and we would be dressed up identically in organdy dresses, with gold barrettes in our hair and little pearls and gold charm bracelets. We'd be all dressed up ready to go, and she'd line us up at the door and say, "Now be good, and never forget that you're a Taylor." Then we'd go out the door, and I would wonder, "Something's wrong here. Is she being sarcastic? How can you be good, because Taylors. . ." Nanny knew who the villains were in the family, and she knew who the good guys were. And the Taylors were the villains. And the Bogerts — my mother and particularly my Grandmother Bogert — were the good guys. So when Nanny said, "Be good, and never forget that you're a Taylor," I never knew how it was possible to be both good and a Taylor because there was always that underbelly of the Taylor family.

Another rule that came through Nanny was, "You were born into wealth, and you will never escape it." And I'd say, "Well, what about the Crash of '29?" And she'd say, "They have safeguards now. The crash will never happen again." And then I'd say, "What about the Russians?" (It was the fifties.) And Nanny would say she didn't think it was possible for the Russians to come, but if they did, that would be the end for all of us.

Nanny had a day off every two weeks. Sometimes she took one of us along on her day off because we were her life. It would be a big event to go to the bus station with Nanny and have a sandwich. It was a big event for her, as well. She had two weeks' vacation in the summer, and we would get an alternate nanny. I would dread those times. Nanny was just so much a part of our everyday life that to have somebody new who didn't know how we did things, and how we got up, and who was allowed to do what, was frightening for us.

There is, with a lot of rich people who as children spent a lot of time with servants, a double bind — there's shame, and there's a bond. There's a sense of intimacy with the servants, and there's also a sense of separation from them, or shame. A number of people I grew up with in Newport were brought up by the chauffeur or the butler. That was their emotional bond, which carried over into their adult life. That's where they would go when they were in trouble. So the role of the servants, whom I loved, set up a conflict and a constant pull within me. I spent a lot of time in the summer in Frederick the butler's house or with May, a maid who had been with the Bogerts forever. I would spend a lot of time in their kitchens. I would dress up in their clothes, and I remember playing in their beds. Those were safe places to be. They were homey. In our own house, we weren't in the kitchen much. The kitchen was in the basement, and that was where the chef was and a whole slew of other people. I remember sort of peeking in there, but we did not hang out in the kitchen. My mother wasn't there baking cookies with me. So there was this other world of the servants, which I probably romanticized. Nanny was also feeding us a romanticized version of her family. I thought that something was happening out there in other people's kitchens that was warm and cozy and safe, that might not be going on in my own house.

But it was much more informal at my house than it was in many other rich households. I saw much more of my mother. I could go to her. In the afternoon, she'd often be sitting in her room, knitting. I felt loved by my mother, and I felt her concern; I felt her being there. But even in my family, children were kept out of the way. That was just the way things were done. When we were in Newport it was much more formal than at home, and I saw much less of my mother. We might be on our way to the beach with Nanny by the time she got up in the morning.

I had a happy life when I was little — until the divorce came. I'd never heard of a divorce because we were so isolated. The divorce was shattering. It meant not just losing my father and my sense of family, it also meant losing the farm where I was born, which was an idyllic place, a sanctuary. And let's not forget what was responsible for this: "Too much money."

On top of that, my mother soon married my first stepfather. Lefty Flynn had had multiple marriages; this was his fifth. He had been disinherited, too. Lefty was a decent man and very grounded, but he had certainly had his share of problems. He struggled with alcoholism throughout his adult life. He took us to live in South Carolina, and life became different for us — much more normal. Nanny took a back seat in our life. Mother cooked dinner, and we had our dinners together.

We all started riding. When I went out on my horse, I would see the shacks where blacks lived, and I saw how awful their living conditions were, but I had been taught to romanticize the poor. I believed in their emotional sense of home and safety. I also felt the injustice of the differences between our family and our help. I remember asking Mother how much she paid Ella, the cook. Mother told me that Ella got thirty dollars a week, and that was top wages. I was just horrified. And I remember when we closed the front door at night, Mother would say, "It's wonderful here. We never have to lock our doors." Once I asked her why, and she said, "If a colored person breaks into your house in South Carolina, the penalty is death."

Nanny was still giving out her messages after we moved to South Carolina. I remember her taking me up to Lefty's closet, opening the door, pointing out a pair of frayed blue pants, and saying, "Now, this is what he brought." And then she'd open the door wider, and there were a lot of new clothes, and she'd say, "And this is what he got." The moral, again, was that men marry you for your money, so look out for gold diggers. That was what this marriage was about, according to Nanny, even though we were picking up something quite different from Mother and Lefty, who were happy. And that was what the previous divorce had been about, according to Nanny. Forget the deeper things about human nature — love and grief. Money ran things. Whenever Lefty had too much to drink, even at times when we might not have noticed anything was going on, Nanny would know, and Nanny would make sure that we knew.

Another of Nanny's big rules was, "You can't be rich and happy." There was also "You can't be rich and good." The rich-and-happy one was never spoken, but it was what I was feeling. There was a lot of guilt, and a feeling that happiness was not easy to come by, particularly if you're rich. You might think you're getting x, y and z, but as Nanny would say, that was not quite what was happening. And then she would bring in her own family as a model. Or "Now look at

Mr. So-and-so. He's a nice man; he goes to work every morning." Of course, Lefty didn't go to work every morning.

Another key person in my childhood was Granny Bogert. She lived a life of tremendous protection, both social and financial. Granny Bogert had her own maid, Lena, who did everything for Granny. Lena ran Granny's bath, dressed her, ironed her stockings, and put the stockings on. Granny had a masseuse come in the morning to give her a massage, and then the chauffeur would take her to the beach. Granny wore silk dresses to the beach. She would come home in the afternoon and crochet, and then she would get ready for dinner. That was Granny's life. Granny was completely taken care of.

What amazes me — because it was not true of her sister, my aunt, and many other people in similar situations — was that Granny was very caring and generous. And Nanny idolized Granny. It was the way Granny spoke to people, the way she spoke to Nanny, the way she cared about her, the way she cared about us. My father used to say she was the most generous person he'd ever met. If she read about someone's misfortune in the paper, or if something happened to a friend, she would go to great lengths to do whatever she could to help. And it was always done in a low-key way and anonymously. You might think that because she was so protected, she would be self-centered, but she wasn't. It's a mystery to me how people develop as they do. She had a generous spirit, and she believed that you were supposed to behave in a low-key manner and be grateful for what you had. And you were supposed to take care of other people. If I was sick, she would get up in the middle of the night. I remember her hovering over me in her nightgown. So I was getting a special message from her — that being rich didn't have to mean that you were spoiled or ungrateful or cold or separated, or any of those other things. It could mean something else.

My father's mother was Grandma Taylor. We went to visit her once a year. We would be dressed up in our identical dresses, and her chauffeur would pick us up, and we'd go have lunch with Grandma. It was not a fun day. We had to sit stiffly in the dining room with her and her nurse and her secretary and her butlers. Lunch was always the same thing. And then we would go for a walk in the gardens, but Grandma would never come. Everything was on her terms, it was very formal, and there was no feeling of connection. She always seemed much richer to me than my other grandmother.

When I was fifteen, my stepfather Lefty died. My mother remarried within a year, and my second stepfather was a world-ranking bridge player. By that time, Nanny had moved down the street and she no longer had the kind of force she had when I was little. My second stepfather broke a lot of the family rules about money. He played with money, and that was something you weren't supposed to do. He also flaunted a high-life style, and that was breaking the rules as well. But we had more fun. The whole family would go on vacation. I remember going to the south of France.

I was becoming more and more aware of drugs and alcohol in the family, and that addictions were not being dealt with, not being confronted. Grief was also being suppressed. A lot of emotional things were being suppressed. I was not getting any of the support that I needed in the social reality that was Newport, or in our life. I felt more and more alienated. And I was very shy — not as sophisticated as my sisters, not as glamorous. I didn't fit in. If I had fit in, I might have made different choices. I felt something was wrong within me. I felt hollow and sad, without knowing what was going on. So I think what happened was that I put myself, almost intentionally, into intense situations, almost to awaken a deadened part of me, or to cut off my exits, or to press the limits. I was looking for a way out.

I was the first girl in the family to finish college. We were never encouraged to go to college. The day after graduation, I found out I was pregnant. I had a botched illegal abortion, which was traumatic for me on every level. Around that time, my mother was planning a trip to the Middle East, and she asked me to come along. We ended up going to the West Bank. It was 1966, before the Six-Day War. While I was in the West Bank, I met Mousa Alami, a Palestinian who was working with refugees in Jericho, and I was very touched by his work. I ended up staying in the West Bank for a year. After the abortion experience I'd been through, working with children was helpful. I lived with Palestinians for the most part, and I started feeling better about myself. I still felt shattered by the abortion because I'd gone against myself in a very deep way, and money wasn't going to solve whatever was basically disturbing to me. I was searching for the things that are truly supportive in life.

After I got back to New York, the Six-Day War came along, and I had all these dreams about the war. Bobby Kennedy was shot around the same time. A lot of things were happening, and they would break me up. I wrote to Mousa Alami, and he asked me to return to the West Bank and do a report. I ended up making several trips to Jericho and writing a report on what was happening. Then I went up to Jerusalem and started working in a crippled children's hospital. That time in my life was a very healing time because it separated me from my family and their traumas.

I had received an inheritance from my grandparents when I was eighteen, and my father died when I was twenty-three, just before I went to the Middle East. I was living very simply and getting paid, so my inheritance was accumulating in my account in New York. My inheritance was maybe a million and a half, and the income from it was more than I ever needed. I wasn't trying to live simply; the lifestyle was just simpler. I felt comfortable and happy.

When I came back to New York, the reality of my stepfather's addiction was evident, and it was another huge crisis. In order to understand the history of addictions in my family, I went to Reality House, a drug rehab program in Harlem. I believe that we usually come to something because we feel ourselves drawn to it, and we feel drawn because something needs to be healed inside ourselves. Most of the men at Reality House had been in prison, and most of the women had been on the street. When I had been there for a couple of days, the director took me aside and said, "If you want to know about this, you need to go through it as if you were an addict." I was in that program for fourteen months.

I felt home free at Reality House. I felt safe in a way that I had not felt safe in my own social environment. The addicts were talking about issues that were not spoken of where I came from. In all fairness, my mother was only trying to protect us, but trying to protect actually promotes fear. Safety is in telling the truth about what's going on in people's lives.

Community was another big thing for me. I didn't feel I had a community in the social world I grew up in, but I found it in the Middle East, where I got involved in a cause, and at Reality House, where I worked in the carpentry shop all day. If I wanted to take a day off, forget it. That was helpful for me. There was no exit on that level. I had to be like everybody else, and that was a relief.

I had been interested in Eastern religions and meditation, and then I went to seminary. I didn't quite know what I wanted to do, but I was drawn to it. I started working with death and dying, and I became a chaplain for a hospice. Around that time, there was a gradual deepening of my attitude towards money. I was moving away from the guilt level and asking questions: How was I living my life? How was I responding? How was I using things?

I was doing a whole reversal of some concepts that are connected with wealth — safety, specialness, and work. It was becoming more and more clear to me that having a great deal of money can impact negatively on both work and relationships. The main spiritual question for me had to do with the sense of separation that I — maybe most of us — felt between myself and God, myself and other people, or myself and my deepest self. It was a question of healing this estrangement, this sense of separation, and coming into a wholeness. Work helps us do that, and relationships help us do that. And if we are separated from those natural ways of healing our sense of separation, then it becomes more difficult.

Money was becoming less real to me and more of a symbol for something, a symbol of great power. But it wasn't real. We think it's real, but in a sense, it's not real, either positively or negatively. It's something to be used. And we think it's real in the sense that it's going to keep us safe, it's going to protect us. People gather money in to keep themselves secure. It was interesting — Reality House was where I felt safe, or working with patients who were dying. So that effort to get more and more money, to protect ourselves from some awful thing out there, like Nanny was saying, that was going to get me if I lost my money, wasn't keeping me safe at all. I was actually feeling the least safety in the places of the most wealth.

I was beginning to understand money not as a demon nor salvation nor protection, but simply as a tool to be used lovingly and creatively. My sense of connection with God was what was going to keep me safe. That's where my safety truly came from. When you're working with the dying, there's a deepening of that sense. As we approach death, from which we have no protection, and from which no amount of money can save us, everything has to be let go of. The only true safety is to be in contact with what is eternal.

Another element I was working with was this thing about being special — that money keeps us separate, one of the elite. For me growing up, being special was very negative. Frederick the butler would talk a lot about Taylor history, and when I'd go over to his house, he'd bring out his pictures of the Taylor family. But instead of feeling special, I felt lacking in self-worth — ashamed, guilty, and isolated. Whether it was the Taylor family history, whether it was Nanny and what she symbolized, whether it was the special clothes, or whatever, as a child, it hadn't felt good to me. It had made me feel like an outsider, and most kids just want their Big Macs and Cokes and blue jeans — whatever is going to make them part of the group.

I was thinking a lot about money and work. Money is supposed to allow you to avoid having to work by the sweat of your brow. Yet living by the sweat of your brow is where the gift is. Work becomes "call," an inner and an outer call, which brings you into a sense of wholeness and puts you in contact with the rest of the world. It gives you the possibility of both inner and outer healing. The purpose of work was not to gain more money or be successful, but to gain your freedom, your connection with community.

Money also gives you a level of choice that other people don't have. When you have to work for survival, choice is taken away from you and you're put into a structure, which was what I was always looking for. When I look back on my twenties, I think if I'd had fewer choices, it might have been easier. I might have moved through the traumas faster because I would have been given structure. When you have a job, you have to get up in the morning, and if you're depressed, too bad. You're pushed into something that you're not too thrilled with, but it is a gift because it's holding you in some fashion, and directing you and bringing you into the world in a way that's helpful.

This question of being present in the world is another fundamental question for me. I didn't know how to come into the world, and my family found it difficult to help me do that. They found it difficult because it hadn't been done for them. They hadn't been given any guidance on how to come into the world. My mother was meant to become a wife and a mother, and if that didn't work out, there wasn't any other possibility for her. For me, coming into the world was connected with coming into a sense of belovedness. And when we don't know our own belovedness as our birthright, then there is all this reaching and grasping onto specialness and symbols of power as substitutes. Belovedness means, not that we are special, because nobody's special, but that we are all precious and beloved. It's everybody's birthright, everybody's inheritance.

This sense of my own belovedness is my true inheritance from my mother and grandmother. My mother, in particular, came to know this belovedness for herself, and I feel that her life was a deepening of that. That was what was real and substantial and enduring. That was what the blessing was all about, and that was what she gave to me. It is what allows me to go out into the world.

I started to think a lot about how to use money lovingly and creatively in the world. What were some of the structures that were unjust? I realized that it didn't help to pretend that those injustices didn't exist. I would have been missing something by ignoring them. I saw that there was something that might be asked of me, that I was not listening to or responding to. What was it? And how did I want to work with it?

A few years ago, I got involved with the Church of the Saviour, an ecumenical church. It provides a safe, nurturing place when you are just beginning to explore and discover how you want to be in the world, to put down little fledgling roots. It's a place to talk and get encouragement and honest feedback — all those things we don't usually get. It was the first time in my life that I had ever talked about some of these things with other people. It was a way to get encouragement in coming out into the world. That was what I had missed, growing up in my family — a place to begin to think, to explore, to try out, to get some honest feedback, to wonder about what my next steps were going to be.

At the Church of the Saviour, I heard about the Ministry of Money, a group that encourages people to examine money issues, both personally and on a global level. I learned that they were organizing a trip to Africa. I was ready to move out into the world, and it was important to me to do that creatively and positively, and without guilt. I had no interest in proselytizing, or bringing the message to anybody.

I didn't see Christianity as the only way, or even the best way. It was just my way. So I ended up going on a three-week trip to Africa with the Ministry of Money, as part of a program called Pilgrimages of Reverse Mission.

One thing I particularly liked was that we were given a lot of room to work at our own speed because there was tremendous culture shock for us. We visited a lot of Mother Theresa's missionaries, the Sisters of Charity, and we worked with them. We were fortunate because they took us right in; we were not left to be observers. I'd walk into a mission, and a Sister would say, "Here's Claire. Will you give her a bath and wash her hair?" Or "Here's a mop." There was a feeling of trust and respect. No one was looking over your shoulder. They just let you be part of their work, and you felt that they were working at a deep spiritual level that had much more to do with a contemplative presence than it had to do with fixing up the world.

It was for me a process of moving from being special to being ordinary, and coming into that everyday, ordinary kind of process and work. You didn't have to be a star, you just had to be there along with everybody else — just join the group. There's a story about Mother Theresa which I have always found powerful. She was taking visitors around her mission, and there was a new Sister, who was picking maggots or something out of somebody's wound, and she was doing it from a distance. Mother took the instrument from her, and said, "Here, you have to do it this way. For this work, you have to get very close." And that's what I see the Ministry of Money doing. They have discovered ways of bringing people from different social, economic, and cultural backgrounds into relationship.

I remember one particularly shattering day that I went to "Garbage City" in Cairo. It's where several hundred thousand Egyptian Copts live. They're the garbage collectors for Cairo, and they literally live *in* the garbage — they sleep, cook, and have their babies there. They're burning garbage all the time, and your eyes sting. I expected to be met by anger, but they were very welcoming. They were so relieved to be looked at and not avoided. I knew a little bit of Arabic, so they told me, "Your money is helpful, but that's not what we need. What we need is to come into a relationship with you. We don't want to be objects of pity or fascination, we need to be seen as human beings. This is something that we both have to share. We have something to contribute to you as well as you to us." That is what relationship is all about. How the money gets used is something different. The coming together, coming into relationship, is the fundamental thing.

The next day, I went to meet the American ambassador. It was just the two of us in his office at the embassy. There we were in this center of power and elegance, but I saw the same look in his eyes that I had seen in the eyes of the people who lived in Garbage City — a longing to be seen and known — and I knew that the same longing was within me, too. It really threw me: why were the two of us there, overlooking the pyramids in this elegant office, and not in Garbage City?

Then I went to stay for the weekend with members of the Masai tribe in Kenya. Everything in that world was up close. I had imagined that I would go there and sit under a tree and write in my journal and have a nice time, but that wasn't what happened. Two guides picked me up in a truck, and I didn't know where I was going. They dressed me in Masai clothes and they put on my clothes. I felt very cared for, but at the same time, it pushed me over my boundaries. They had never had a white visitor before. It was like show-and-tell; every freckle was counted, my hair was brushed — everything. There were twelve kids in the family and two wives, and I slept with a daughter. It was almost more than I could handle — too much intimacy, too strange and too close. It was extraordinary to be put right into the midst of another way of relating, and I had no defense against it. I just had to be carried along. It was very, very powerful.

My response to that visit with the Masai goes back to issues of money and families. Being with the Masai was the exact opposite of my early experience. In my family, there was so much separation between parents and children, there were so many boundaries. It was a rare day when Mother brushed my hair; Nanny was the one who did that. We rarely sat down at the table together, and when my sisters and I were older and we were finally allowed to eat with my parents, the focus was more on manners. There was no easy emotional back and forth.

Letting go of my physical space and my privacy has been the hardest thing for me. In the middle of the night, in that Masai hut, when I was lying in bed with the Masai girl, I thought I was going to lose it and start screaming.

Coming back from that kind of intense third-world experience, I had to ask myself: how do I respond to others? Generosity isn't about just hurling your money away, getting rid of your money. We all have to answer this individually, and for some people it might be absolutely the right thing to give away all of their money, and for others, maybe it isn't. The question for me is always one of motivation. Why am I doing this? And the question that keeps coming back is: Am I faithful, and to what? Am I faithful to the deepest sense of myself, to my understanding of life purpose, and to what is the bedrock for me? It's such a long process. It's a life-long deepening, and each situation is different from the one before.

What are rich people asking for? They don't want to be asked just for their money; they want to be asked to give a part of themselves and to be brought into that giving in a meaningful way. That is for the benefit of both sides in the relationship. How can we do philanthropy in a way that feels right and creative and loving for each person?

Money has a kinder face for me now. I've had to work through a lot of guilt and shame before I could see the advantages of wealth. Now I'm beginning to feel grateful in ways that I couldn't have before. Money has given me dream time. It means that I can sit here with you now. I've had time in my life, whether we're talking about an afternoon here or there, or longer periods of time, to develop my inner spiritual life. Not that you can't do that otherwise, but if you've got a lot of financial pressures and a tremendous amount of work, you can barely get the day finished. But I can have quiet time in the morning or evening. I can take walks. My challenge is to bring that inner world into the outer world. That is what's most difficult for me. You could put me out on a rock forever and I'd be content, but to move out into relationship in the world with people, with work, is the challenge.

# *Afterword*

We hope you have been touched by the honesty, the struggles, and the triumphs contained in these narratives. As we collected the interviews for this project, we were consistently struck by the sheer power of storytelling — its power to uncover meaning and coherence in seemingly random experiences, its power to diminish shame made worse by silence, its power to connect listener to speaker in compassion and interest. After hearing more than forty life stories from inheritors, we are convinced that storytelling can heal.

We want to offer our heartfelt thanks to the people who so willingly and courageously shared their time, their lives, and their secrets with us. We want them to know what a gift they have given by breaking the taboo against talking about the mixed blessings of inherited wealth. By revealing the details of their private challenges — so particular and yet so representative — they  pave the way for other heirs to undertake the same journey out of guilt and ignorance into the kind of empowerment that makes wealth a genuine blessing, both to oneself and to one's world.

If you have heard in these voices bits and pieces of your own experience,  take comfort in the knowledge that you are not alone. In fact, there are so many other people who can identify with the uncomfortable feelings you may have felt as you read this book — embarrassment, anger, self-doubt, confusion — that there are now entire networks in place designed to support and educate heirs. Inheritors can find conferences, consultants, therapists, newsletters, and books — all geared toward addressing the troublesome issues that accompany the process of inheritance. Our revised resource directory lists many of these services.

Finally, you can also do us a favor by passing this book on to friends who might benefit from its insights and revelations. Despite the fine efforts of various support groups and networks to foster open communication among heirs, the world of inheritors still operates largely as a kind of underworld. The rumor mill churns with whispered speculations about the pedigree and net worth of suspected heirs. Predictably, such secrecy only contributes to the feeling many heirs have that by coming into money, they have committed some vague crime.

We feel strongly that if you share with your families and friends the stories contained in this book, you will be helping to dismantle the rumor mill and to build an atmosphere for heirs that is free of shame and secrecy. We thank you so much for your interest in this project and your help in circulating it.

# Resource Directory

## 1. NETWORKS, SERVICES & CONFERENCES

*A Territory Resource (ATR)* 603 Steward Street, #1007, Seattle, WA
98101  206/624-4081. www.atrfoundation.org
A public foundation funding social change projects in the Northwest.
Educational events for donors.

*Comfort Zone*  P.O. Box 400336, North Cambridge, MA 02140
617/441-5567 hewat@tiac.net
Supports progressive young people with wealth in using resources in
alignment with their values.

*Funding Exchange Network* 666 Broadway, Suite 500, New York,
NY 10025  212/529-5300.
A national network of alternative foundations committed to
funding progressive grassroots organizations. Some member
organizations hold conferences for people with wealth. For
more information about FEX member groups: www.fex.org

> *Appalachian Community Fund*, Knoxville, TN
> *Bread and Roses Community Fund*, Philadelphia, PA
> *Chinook Fund*, Denver, CO
> *Crossroads Fund*, Chicago, IL
> *Fund for Southern Communities*, Atlanta, GA
> *Haymarket People's Fund*, Boston, MA
> *Headwaters Fund*, Minneapolis, MN
> *Liberty Hill Foundation*, Santa Monica, CA
> *McKenzie River Gathering Foundation*, Portland, OR
> *North Star Fund*, New York, NY
> *The People's Fund*, Honolulu, HI
> *Three Rivers Community Fund*, Pittsburgh, PA
> *Vanguard Public Foundation*, San Francisco, CA
> *Wisconsin Community Fund*, Madison, WI

*Family Firm Institute* 221 N. Beacon Street, Boston, MA 02135
617/789-4200 www.ffi.org
A network of advisors to family businesses. Annual conferences.

*Family Office Exchange* 137 North Oak Park Avenue, Suite 210,
Oak Park, IL 60301 708/848-2030 www.familyoffice.com Provides
research, education and networking to family offices.

*Heirs* Box 292, Villanova, PA 19085 610/527-6260
stancedar@aol.com
Information and occasional conferences for trust beneficiaries.

*Institute for Private Investors* 74 Trinity Place, New York, NY
10000 212/693-1300 IPI@MEMBERLINK.NET
A networking and educational resource for wealthy families and their
advisors. Annual program in private wealth management.

*The Legacy Companies, LLC* 1150 Hancock Street, Quincy, MA
02169 617/689-0777 legacy@tiac.net
Creators of The Legacy Planning System™, a values-based approach
to family wealth transfer.

*Ministry of Money* 11315 Neelsville Church Road, Germantown, MD 20876-4147 301/428-9560 minmon@erols.com
A Christian perspective on wealth. Workshops and pilgrimages.

*National Association of Family Wealth Counselors* 20 Circle Drive,
Franklin, IN 46131 317/736-6468 www.nafwc.org
A network of values-based family wealth planners.

*The Philanthropic Initiative* 77 Franklin Street, Boston, MA 02110
617/338-2590 get2us@tpi.org
Philanthropic design and management for individuals, families and
corporations.

*Resourceful Women* Presidio Building 1016, San Francisco, CA
94129-0423 415/561-6520 reswomen@aol.com Financial and
philanthropic education, and personal support for women of wealth.

*Threshold Foundation* P.O. Box 29903, San Francisco, CA 94129-0903 415/561-6400 awilson@tides.org
A membership organization of 300 individuals with inherited and earned wealth who engage in progressive grantmaking. Threshold is also a forum where members can dialogue about social, financial, spiritual and personal matters.

*The Wealth Conservancy, Inc.* 1919 14th Street, Suite 319, Boulder, CO 80302 303/444-1919 Helps inheritors integrate, understand and have control over their financial resources. Annual workshops: "Inherited Wealth and You."

*Programs offered by banks and trust companies*

*There is a growing trend for banks and trust companies to sponsor seminars for their high-net-worth clients—sometimes by invitation only. Most seminars focus on wealth management, although some also examine the social and emotional challenges of wealth. Check with large banks in your area.*

*Bankers Trust Company* c/o Peter Scaturro, 280 Park Avenue, New York, NY 10017 212/454-1504 peter.k.scaturro@bankerstrust.com

*Bessemer Trust* c/o Karen A.G. Loud, 630 5th Avenue, New York, NY 10111 212/708-9100 loud@bessemer.com

*Harris Trust & Savings Bank* c/o Mary Ann Fernandez, 111 West Monroe Street, Chicago, IL 60603 312/461-6477 maryann.fernandez@harrisbank.com

*Northern Trust Company* c/o Rick Waddell, 50 South La Salle Street, Chicago, IL 60675 312/630-6000 fhw@notes.ntrs.com

*Resource Companies* c/o Rod Boren, International Centre, Suite 30, 900 2nd Avenue South, Minneapolis, MN 612/338-7881

*UMB* Private Client Services, c/o Cindy Thurston, 1010 Grand, Kansas City, MO 64106 816/860-7729 c_thurston@umb.com

## 2. PROFESSIONAL ADVISORS

*These consultants work within a holistic framework. They consider the emotional and financial aspects of inheritance inseparable, and their work is values-based.*

*Judy Barber* Family business consultant, licensed marriage and family counselor, 1515 Fourth Street, Suite B, Napa, CA 94554 707/255-6254

*Olivia Boyce-Abel* Family lands consultant, 1003 Smith Grade, Santa Cruz, CA 95060 408/469-9223

*Joanie Bronfman* Psychologist, 1731 Beacon Street, Apt. 517, Brookline, MA 02146 617/262-1754

*Jacqueline Carleton* Psychologist, 115 East 92nd Street, New York, NY 10128 212/987-4969

*Sally Donaldson* Psychologist, New York, NY 212/929-4738

*Scott Fithian* Estate planner, 1150 Hancock Street, 3rd floor, Quincy, MA 02169 617/689-3224

*Tracy Gary* Philanthropic advisor, P.O. Box 428, Ross, CA 94957 415/461-5539

*Lee Hausner* Psychologist, Doud, Hausner & Associates, 14724 Ventura Blvd, # 704, Sherman Oaks, CA 91403 818/539-2267

*Terry Hunt* Psychologist, 214 Market Street, Brighton, MA 02135 617/787-3511

*Valerie Jacobs* MFCC, Family Philanthropy Resource, 7801 Mission Center Court, # 200, San Diego, CA 92108 619/295-5088

*Jennifer Ladd* Philanthropic advisor, 245 Main Street, #207, Northampton, MA 01060 413/585-9709

*John L. Levy* Wealth counselor, 842 Autumn Lane, Mill Valley, CA 94941 415/383-3951

*Olivia Mellan* Psychotherapist, The Washington Therapy Guild, 2607 Connecticut Avenue, Washington, D.C. 20008   202/483-2660 (ext. 4)

*Jessie O'Neill* M.A., 8940 North Upper River Road, River Hills, WI 53217 414/351-8442

*Dennis Pearne* Psychologist, 9 Alexander Avenue, Belmont, MA 02178-4802 617/484-0013

*Kito Peters* Psychologist, P.O. Box 752, Placitas, NM 87043 505/867-6715

*Sharon Rich* Investment advisor, 76 Townsend Road, Belmont, MA 02178 617/489-3601

*John Ward* Family business consultant, The Family Business Consulting Group, Inc., 1111 Forest Avenue, Evanston, IL 60202 847/475-3000

*Peter White* Wealth consultant, 201 West Minnesota Avenue, DeLand, FL 32720 904/943-9811

*Thayer Willis* Psychologist, 340 Oswego Pointe Drive, Suite 205, Lake Oswego, OR 97034-3230 503/636-1179

*Kathy Wiseman* Family business consultant, Working Systems, 2000 L Street, Suite 522, Washington, D.C. 20036 202/659-2222

## 3. RECOMMENDED BOOKS & ARTICLES

Alexander, Michael, *How to Inherit Money: A Guide to Making Good Financial Decisions After Losing Someone You Love* (Franklin Lakes, NJ: Career Press, 1998).

Bronfman, Joanie, *The Experience of Inherited Wealth: A Social-Psychological Perspective* (Ann Arbor, MI: University Microfilms, 1987).

Coles, Robert, *Privileged Ones: The Well-Off and the Rich in America* (Boston: Little Brown, 1977).

Comfort Zone, *Money Talks. So Can We. Resources for People in their 20s.* Comfort Zone, Box 336, Cambridge, MA 02140.

Hausner, Lee, *Children of Paradise: Successful Parenting for Prosperous Families* 1-800/834-1911

## *From The Inheritance Project/Trio Press:*

"The Inheritor's Inner Landscape: How Heirs Feel" 14 pages.
Explores the emotional challenges heirs face in their efforts to come to terms with their wealth.

"Inheritors and Work: The Search for Purpose" 50 pages.
Not having to support themselves often leads heirs down dead-end streets. Explores how heirs come to terms with this situation.

*The Legacy of Inherited Wealth: Interviews with Heirs* 186 pages.
Candid interviews with inheritors offer an inside view of the unique blessings and challenges of inheriting enough wealth to make paid work a matter of choice. Extensive resource section.

*Like a Second Mother: Nannies and Housekeepers in the Lives of Wealthy Children* 328 pages.
Wealthy adults recall the caregivers who loved and nurtured them as children; caregivers recall the children they helped raise. Available after June 1999.

"Passing Wealth Along to Our Children: Emotional Complexities of Estate Planning" 26 pages.
Follows a fictional family through the complexities of estate planning to illustrate the dilemmas that arise in leaving wealth to descendants.

"Wealth Counseling: A Guide for Therapists and Inheritors" 18 pages.
Dennis Pearne, a psychologist, discusses how to work with issues most likely to be obstacles for heirs: guilt, shame, financial paralysis, and fear.

"Working with Inherited Wealth Clients: A Guide for Professional Advisors" 8 pages.
Familiarizes advisors with emotional difficulties facing inherited-wealth clients and suggests strategies for making communication more effective.

> *To order from The Inheritance Project/Trio Press:*
> *www.inheritance-project.com*
> *Or contact us directly: kgibson112@aol.com*
> *540/953-3977 (voice mailbox)*
> *fax 549/951-4020*
> *The Inheritance Project*
> *P.O. Box 933*
> *Blacksburg, VA 24063-0933*

Levy, John L. has several short articles available at no charge. For more information: 842 Autumn Lane, Mill Valley, CA 94941 415/383-3951.

Mogil, Christopher, & Anne Slepian, *We Gave Away a Fortune: Stories of People Who Have Devoted Themselves and Their Wealth to Peace, Justice and a Healthy Environment* More than Money, 2244 Alder Street, Eugene, OR 97405 541/343-2420.

O'Neill, Jessie, *The Golden Ghetto: The Psychology of Affluence* (Center City, MN: Hazelden, 1997).

Rottenberg, Dan, *The Inheritor's Handbook: A Definitive Guide for Beneficiaries* (New York: Bloomberg, 1998).

Stanny, Barbara, *Prince Charming Isn't Coming: How Women Get Smart About Money* (New York: Viking, 1997).

Steinem, Gloria, "The Masculinization of Wealth," in *Moving Beyond Words* (New York: Simon & Schuster, 1994).
First printed in *Ms.* as "The Trouble with Rich Women," 1986.

Stone, Deanne, Mudita Nisker & Dan Clurman, *Money Disagreements: How to Talk About Them* Communication Options, 396 61st Street, Oakland, CA 94618

Stone, Deanne, & Barbara Stanny, *Choosing and Managing Financial Professionals: A Guide for Women Investors*
Resourceful Women, 3543 18th Street, San Francisco, CA 94110
415/431-5677

## 4. NEWSLETTERS

*Family Money: A Quarterly Commentary on the Unspoken Issues Related to Wealth* 1515 Fourth Street, Suite B, Napa, CA 94559
707/255-6254

*Fiduciary Fun* c/o Heirs, Box 292, Villanova, PA 19085
610/527-6260

*Ministry of Money Newsletter* 11315 Neelsville Church Road, Germantown, MD 20876-4147 301/428-9560

*More Than Money: Exploring the Personal, Political and Spiritual Impact of Wealth in Our Lives* 2244 Alder Street, Eugene, OR 97405 541/343-2420

# Questions for Reflection

*These are some of the questions we asked when we talked with heirs.*

### CHILDHOOD AND FAMILY

1. When did you first realize that you were different from your peers in terms of wealth? How old were you when you first realized this difference? How did you feel about it?

2. Did your parents talk about the family's wealth? Was it okay for you to talk about it? Was it okay to ask questions? When was it not okay to talk about it?

3. What were the "rules" or "messages" in your family in relation to wealth? For example: Don't talk about the family's wealth; never invade principal; don't display your wealth; remember your position in society and as a representative of your family.

4. What class differences did you become aware of? At what age?

5. How did the wealth come into your family? Did it come from one side of your family? Both sides? Was the money earned, inherited, invested, etc.? How long has there been wealth in your family?

6. What kind of work did your parents do? Did your mother work outside the home? What were your family's messages concerning work for women?

7. Were there servants in your household? What was your relationship to them? Who was your primary caregiver? How did you feel about the servants?

8. What kinds of luxuries and privileges did you and your family have? In what ways did your family not allow themselves — or you — luxuries or privileges (for example: public school instead of private; hand-me-downs)?

9. Did anyone teach you how to handle money? If so, how?

10. How did your family's wealth affect you when you were a teenager?

11. What were your parents' expectations for you? Were their expectations for your siblings the same or different? Were there gender differences?

## GENERAL QUESTIONS '

1. What kinds of difficulties have you found in having wealth? How have you dealt with them? What and/or who was helpful to you in dealing with these obstacles?

2. How have you made use of the opportunities your wealth has offered you?

3. Have your attitudes about your money and its role in your life changed over the years? What caused your perspective to change?

4. What does having wealth mean to you?

5. Do you think of yourself as wealthy? Would you like to have more money or less? Why?

6. Do you feel like the money is yours? Why or why not?

7. Do you work for money? If so, why? Is working for money an issue for you? Do you work as a volunteer? What does "work" mean for you?

8. Do you know how much money you have? If you don't know, what has prevented you from finding out?

9. How much control do you have over your money — principal, income, the way it is invested, etc.? If your money is managed by someone else, what relationship do you have to that person or institution? Would you like to change the way your money is managed? How would you like it to change?

10. Do you think you have been used by others because you are wealthy? Have you ever felt resented? Envied?

11. Have you ever tried to conceal your wealth? Why?

12. How has wealth affected your close relationships? What are the positive and the negative aspects of your money in these relationships?

13. If you have children, do you plan to give them money? Why or why not? What do you want to teach them about their wealth and how to use it? If you have already given them money, how has it

affected them so far? If you have step-children, what challenges does your wealth pose in your relationships to them?

14. How much money do you give away? How do you decide how much to give and to whom, or to which organizations?

15. If you could start your life over, would you choose to be wealthy by inheritance?

# PUBLICATIONS FROM THE INHERITANCE PROJECT, INC.

*The Legacy of Inherited Wealth: Interviews with Heirs*   $17.95
($14.95 + $3.00 for shipping & handling)

*The Inheritor's Inner Landscape*   $12.00
(shipping and handling included)
This 29-page monograph explores the emotional challenges which heirs may face in their efforts to come to terms with their wealth. Drawing extensively on anecdotes and advice from inheritors, it maps out the psychic terrain which heirs often travel — its quagmires as well as its vistas. A resource directory is included.

*Passing Wealth Along: A Guided Tour*   $12.00
(shipping and handling included)
This 28-page monograph introduces readers to the emotional complexities of creating trusts and wills. It follows the story of Stan and Nancy Blackman — fictional affluent parents — through their decision-making process as they work with a lawyer to determine how best to leave money to their three children. This article is useful both to wealthy parents as well as to the estate attorneys and financial planners with whom they work. A bibliography is included.

### TO ORDER ANY OF THESE PUBLICATIONS

Please send a check, made out to The Inheritance Project, Inc., to:

The Inheritance Project, Inc.
3291 Deer Run Road
Blacksburg, VA 24060

*Virginia residents:* Please add 4.5% sales tax to your total.

*Canadian orders:* Please send, in Canadian dollars, $20.95 ($17.95 + $3.00 for shipping & handling) for *The Legacy of Inherited Wealth* and $12.00 (shipping & handling included) for each of the two monographs, to:

The Inheritance Project, Inc.
5280 Green Street, Box 27063
Halifax, Nova Scotia  B3H 4M8

Bulk rates are available. For information, call (703) 552-8436 or fax (703) 951-4020.

Thank you for your interest.